No More Unclaimed Promises

Purpose Driven Women Share Empowering Messages of How They Embraced and Stood on the Promises in God's Word, and How You Can, Too!

A Compilation by Dr. Ranelli A. Williams, CPA

Foreword by Donna Izzard

© 2021 Dr. Ranelli A. Williams

Scripture is taken from The Holy Bible, King James Version (KJV), Copyright (c) 1996 unless otherwise stated.

Printed in the United States of America

Paperback ISBN: 978-1-7335065-6-4
E-Book ISBN: 978-1-7335065-7-1

No More Unclaimed Promises

Foreword
By Donna Izzard

If you ever had a doubt as to what a promise is, what a promise looks like, or if a promise is real or not, then all you need to do is to read the stories reflected in this profound work compiled by Dr. Ranelli A. Williams.

When reflecting on a promise from God, we can taste, chew, swallow, bring it up again, taste some more, and repeat this process. God will never break His promises to us because we are children of the promise. The Holy Spirit that dwells within us is the spirit of promise.

God's promises are yes and amen. God is a promise keeper, and we can reap the promises of God. Man often lies, but GOD does not lie, and His promises reflect that if we would just believe. In Jeremiah 1:12 (NKJV), God said, "For I am ready to perform my word."

The chapters in "No More Unclaimed Promises" help us build up our faith, as we know that God's word cannot fail. God's word is clear, stating that "heaven and earth will pass away, but my words will never pass away" (Matthew 24:35, NIV). We can stand on God's word and recognize obstacles as "challenging opportunities." These chapters help us believe and let us know that God loves us. They help us understand the power and purpose of God's promises. I call God's promises "unstoppable." These chapters allow us to comprehend the notion that God and only God can give us a promise that is reflective in our lives. The promises of God help us to build our individual lives, build our families, and build our future. It's time to journey towards a destination that awaits you as you read through the chapters of this awesome and timely book.

Author, International Speaker, Women Empowerment Leader, and Multiple Revenue Streams Strategist **Donna Hicks Izzard** is a woman with vision. As intuitive as she is inspirational, she helps highly successful corporate professionals and faith-based leaders to blend their expertise and brilliance into profitable, passion-fueled businesses while maintaining their full-time careers and ministries. She is a woman with a gift.

For several years, she was the business manager for a former "White House Ambassador." As a training and development professional in the legal industry with over 30+ years' experience, she has been a mentor to women from different cultures and backgrounds. Donna was tagged as one of the top coaches to watch by the Huffington Post and most recently recognized as one of the Top 30 Black Global leaders by Impact.

Introduction
By Dr. Ranelli A. Williams, CPA

It was May 2021, as I was anticipating my next move in business, whether I should totally shut down one of my businesses to give full focus to the other, God jolted my memory that I need to focus on His promises and the call that He placed on my life. The struggle for my time and resources were presenting a challenge, and I was ready to abandon the call rather than turn to Him for the answer and direction. What I forgot was that not because I was called means that the journey would be a smooth one, but what it means is that my destination is promised and secure.

You see, I was brought up in the church, and like many Christians, I forgot that while blessings are a gift from God like salvation is, there are pre-requisites along the journey. The Bible tells us to believe in the Lord, Christ Jesus, and we will be saved. In the same way, when we believe in His promises, that belief moves us to action, even uncomfortable action, which takes us in the direction of the promised gift, and it is in those actions that the blessing is manifested in our lives. So, my beautiful purpose-driven woman of God, I invite you to stand on God's promises found in His word and take the action He is calling you to.

If you have a need, turn to Philippians 4:19 (ESV), which tells you, "And my God will supply every need of your according to his riches in glory in Christ Jesus." That is a promise. God promised to supply all your needs and not some of your needs. Do you believe it? Are you claiming it for your life?

If you are worried about your future, stop worrying. Jeremiah 29:11 (NIV) states, "For I know the plans I have for you, declares the Lord, plans to prosper you and not to harm you, plans to give you hope and a future." God promised you hope and prosperity, so why worry? You are called to believe and accept the promise.

If you have a challenge that you are facing, instead of succumbing to that challenge, remember Isaiah 41:10 (KJV), which says, "Fear not, for I am with you; be not dismayed, for I am thy God. I will strengthen thee; yea, I will help thee; yea, I will uphold thee with the right hand of my righteousness." That scripture is confirmation that you have all that you need once you are in Christ. You have nothing to fear because He promised to give you strength and help you through whatever it is that you are going through.

If you face the decision of, how do I return a faithful tithe when I am living paycheck to paycheck, as my friend Donna Izzard would say, "who do you believe?" Malachi 3:10-12 challenges us to prove God by being faithful, and when we do, He will pour out such a blessing on us, we will not have room to receive it. Do you believe God?

One of my favorite promises as a money breakthrough business coach is found in Isaiah 60:5 (NIV) as God declares to ME personally as a descendant of Abraham, the father of all nations, "Then you will look and be radiant, your heart will throb and swell with joy; the wealth on the seas will be brought to you, to you the riches of the nations will come." This promise is for all of us. Yes, there is enough for all of us because when He blesses me, I can bless someone else, and if we all have a heart to pay it forward, do you see how the blessings can be in perpetuity?

There are so many other scripture-promises that you can go to when you are facing a roadblock or a difficult situation or decision. And through the messages shared in this book that you would see the hand of God moving in the lives of these women and know that you too are His child and heir to His promises and His kingdom. Believe it, accept it, and receive it.

Sheltered! Protected!
By Hazel D. Adams Riley

*The angel of the Lord encamps all around those who fear Him,
and delivers them."*
Psalm 34:7 NKJV

*"When you pass through the waters, I will be with you; and
through the rivers, they shall not overflow you. When you walk
through the fire, you shall not be burned, nor shall the flame
scorch you."*
Isaiah 43: 2

Hurricanes, Earthquakes, Volcanoes! Growing up in the Caribbean, I had heard those words, but to me, they were natural phenomena that affected persons in distant lands, or maybe they were terms in the geography books. However, in my adult life, they became very real to me, and I thank God that He sheltered and protected me through them all.

I had heard my parents and other adults talking about Hurricane Donna, and every year they would get ready for the "hurricane season." They checked the roofs, made sure the windows were in good repair, stocked up on dry goods and tinned items such as biscuits, sardines, and sausages. It was an exciting time. Occasionally, we would hear the name of an approaching storm, and excitement would rise, only to fall when it passed by, giving us a wide berth. I was taught a little poem that was a reminder of the possible impact of a hurricane or tropical storm.

"June too soon, July stand by,
August lookout it must,
September remember,
October all over."

9

As an adult with a family of my own, including a two-year-old daughter, I faced the wrath of Hurricane Hugo. On September 15, 1989, word reached us that a storm was approaching the Leeward Islands, and people should get ready.

Hurricane

At first, the path was not clear, but by the next day, Montserrat, the island where I lived, was in the cone of uncertainty. I prayed and claimed the promise, *"The angel of the Lord encamps all around those who fear Him and delivers them."*

I jumped into action. I called around to ensure that friends and associates, especially the elderly knew that a storm was approaching. By early Saturday morning, there was no doubt in my mind that it was coming. We were going to be impacted. Normally on a Saturday morning, my family and I would go to church to worship God, leaving all work behind, and but not this Saturday. I double-checked to ensure that documents (passports, birth, and school certificates) were secured in zip-lock plastic bags. I had the necessary items for my family of five (water, non-perishable food items, bread, matches, flashlights with extra batteries, and more water). I encouraged my husband to double-check windows and doors at home and our business.

After that was done, my husband and I went into town and checked on our brethren, who were boarding up our church building while others secured the homes of the elderly. Like Noah's family in the Bible, we were ridiculed by some onlookers. They said we had no faith, but we knew that God had given man wisdom to be able to track the path of the storm, and it was approaching. At home, we parked our vehicles as close to the house as we could since we had no garage. I prepared and fed my family a hot meal that evening, not knowing when we would eat again. I showered, dressed in casual street clothes, placed my shoes at the foot of the bed where I could find them easily, and went to bed, not to sleep but to wait. As Hugo went from a Tropical Storm to a Category Three Hurricane and then headed straight for Montserrat, we were glued to our radio.

All night and into the next morning, the winds howled, then there was silence as the storm passed overhead. We had been warned not to go outside because the winds would soon return from the opposite direction, and it did. The song "Pray When the Storm Clouds Gather Overhead" played in my mind, and I prayed along with many around the island, I later learned. That was the longest and most terrifying night of my life. The commotion outside was unbelievable. The rain pelted the house; the wind roared like a madman and ripped our roof from over our heads as my family cowered in a clothes closet. From within the house, I could see the branches of a massive tamarind tree next door twisting and turning as though an invisible hand was trying to yank it from the ground. The storm pounded the island well into the next day. It took hours before we could make our way downstairs to a vacant apartment. Through it all, the Lord sheltered and protected my family.

When the clouds lifted a couple of days later, and we were able to venture out, the morning light revealed a most devastating sight. We could see for miles around. All the houses around us no longer had roofs, it seemed. Debris was strewn all around, and the trees and hillside were bare and blackened.

Hurricane Hugo had passed directly over the island as a category four hurricane. It left my home partially destroyed, along with over 90% of the island's infrastructure. The communication system was badly damaged, so we had no way to communicate with our loved ones at home and abroad. Thank God we never lost communication with our Heavenly Father. As a result of downed trees, debris, and wires, it was days before we could move around to check on relatives, friends, and our business places. Sadly, we learned that several persons had lost their lives, but we gave God thanks for sheltering and protecting us. He had heard our prayers. His communication system was never down.

About a week later, as part of the fact-finding mission to assess the damage, Government officials toured the island. The Minister of Education, Mrs. Annie Dyer Howe, visited the Montserrat Seventh-day Adventist Community School, where I was the principal. As we looked at the school building, we recognized that it had only lost a few shingles; she said words that thrill me even today, *"The angel of the Lord was standing over your school."* All around us, buildings were without roofs, and walls had even been broken, but our school stood intact. Some designated shelters had to be evacuated at the height of the storm, as they suffered damage. It took us years to rebuild our homes, lives, and country, but God had sheltered His people.

Just when we thought that Montserrat was on the way to recovery, another tragedy struck. The Soufriere Hills Volcano came rumbling back to life-destroying life as we knew it.

Volcanic Eruption

On the afternoon of July 18, 1995, I, along with the residents on Montserrat, learned that residents in and around the capital of Plymouth had been hearing a loud roaring sound like an airplane in the sky above the mountain range known as Gages Mountain. The sound continued all day, but no airplane had been sighted. Something like ash from a wood fire began falling from the sky, but there was no sign of a fire. Residents were concerned. I was curious. As the evening progressed, people got more and more concerned. What was going on? They wondered. I got into my vehicle and headed into the town to see and hear for myself. People were heading in the opposite direction.

The local radio station, Radio ZJB, confirmed that evening the start of volcanic activity on the island, and panic set in. Scientists came from overseas to monitor the activity. Unknown to us, they had been on watch for volcanic activity for months, alerted by the swarm of earthquakes that had preceded the eruption.

The scientists announced that a vent had opened in the mountain. Over time more and more vents opened, lava domes grew and collapsed, and light ash then heavy ash continued to fall. On August 21, 1995, a large eruption blanketed Plymouth in a thick ash cloud, completely blocking out the morning sun and causing darkness for about fifteen minutes. Many thought that the end had come. Parents thought that they would never see their children again. We prayed and claimed God's promises for protection.

Later an explosive eruption sent huge ballistic blocks almost one and a half miles away, destroying houses in the village of Long Ground. This was an early indication of the power of the awakening volcano. It triggered the first of many evacuations of southern Montserrat and the wearing of ash masks. The town and villages were evacuated as a precautionary measure, but not without much protest. People left home with an overnight bag, never to return home again. Schools and churches became temporary accommodation or shelters for persons who had been forced to flee their homes.

At night the mountain glowed, and red-hot rocks cascaded down the mountainside, a beautiful but deadly sight. It attracted crowds, who viewed in awe from a distance kept back by police at barricades which kept appearing all over the island. A foul-smelling sulfurous gas was emitted, a constant reminder of the presence of a deadly volcano in the mountains.

Phreatic eruptions began. These are "steam-driven explosions that occur when water beneath the ground or on the surface is heated by magma, lava, hot rocks, or new volcanic deposits." Pyroclastic flows became the order of the day. These are fast-moving currents of hot gas and volcanic matter that flow along the ground away from a volcano, making their way to the sea. Large mushroom clouds rose majestically in the sky. We thank God that these rivers of fire moved away from the central occupied portion of the island. Pebbles fell onto homes in the occupied "so-called" safe zone miles away, necessitating the wearing of hard hats.

On July 25, 1997, a major dome collapsed at the Soufrière Hills Volcano and took the life of 19 persons. Most of these perished when Pyroclastic flows of super-heated gases and rocks swept down all sides of the mountain, trapping them and almost

13

consuming their bodies. Though it was a sad and scary time, I knew that God had promised, *"Yea, though I walk through the valley of the shadow of death, I will fear no evil."* The promise *"When you walk through the fire, you shall not be burned, nor shall the flame scorch you" still* applied to me.

Schools, churches, and businesses in about two-thirds of the island closed permanently, and the economy ground to a standstill. Forced to leave their homes with the bare necessities, living in cramped shelters in schools, tents, vehicles, or with relatives or friends, having little or no privacy and no possessions, and seeing no future at home, thousands accepted the offer of life in the United Kingdom. Families were torn apart. Many parents made the tough decision for mothers to take the children abroad to pursue educational opportunities, while the men stayed on the island to rebuild and preserve the island for their families.

Dear Friend, are you in a situation and feel like there is no way out? Whatever you are going through right now, remember that you serve a God whose Word is filled with treasures and promises, like the ones I claimed. He is a strong tower and has promised to be yours too. YES! He is able to deliver you too. The words of the song "Sheltered, Protected No Evil Can Harm Me" are as true today as the day they were written. Know that God has promised to shelter and protect you and to be with you when you pass through water, fire, and every situation, even the COVID pandemic.

Heavenly Father, you are our refuge and strength; you have been my help in times of trouble. I thank you for showing up and showing off in my life and the lives of your people. I commit the one reading these words to you, asking that you will give him or her an experience that they too will be able to talk of your protection. Thank you, Lord! Amen!

Hazel D. Adams Riley

Hazel D. Adams Riley is the First Elder in the New Carmel Seventh-day Adventist Church on Montserrat, W.I. A regular presenter on the Signs of the Times Radio and The Adventist Voice programs on Radio Montserrat, she has served the Church in many areas on both St. Kitts and Montserrat.

She migrated to Montserrat from her homeland St. Kitts in 1983 to serve as Principal of the Montserrat Seventh-day Adventist Community School. Following the fatal eruption at the Soufriere Hills Volcano in 1997, she evacuated with her daughter to St. Kitts, where she lectured at the Clarence Fitzroy Bryant College in the Teacher Education Division. Returning to Montserrat in 2005, she worked in Public Service Reform as a lecturer at the Montserrat Community College and as a journalist before joining her family-run business, the Emerald Emporium Ltd, as Associate Manager.

In response to the question in Exodus 4:2, "What is that in your hand?" she uses her voice and her pen (devices) to proclaim God's last day message.

Do Not Quit on Yourself!
By Dr. Marine E. Bryan

*"Do not be afraid or discouraged because of this vast army, for
the battle is not yours, but God's."*
2 Chronicles 20:15b

"I can do all things through Christ who strengthens me."
Philippians 3: 14

Although I set out on a heightened positive note with approval
from God to complete my dissertation program, it appeared dull
throughout the years. My dissertation journey was flustered with
situations such as a broken relationship, single parenting, negative
criticism, and intimidation from my Chair to influence my
potential, which discouraged me. I gave up on my academic goal
a few times because I felt alone and very distant from God with
my struggles. What was frustrating was that for every setback,
there were significant turning points; however, I was bombarded
by new struggles due to the Covid 19 pandemic and deeper
despair due to the loss of my parents. The scriptures above
motivated me to hold on to God's unchanging provision of
support and belief that propelled me to complete my dissertation
successfully.

Dear God, help me not to be disquieted and cast down as I faced
my crucibles, causing setbacks for completing my dissertation
program. Due to human nature, sometimes, with the wavering of
my faith, I felt like quitting on my heartfelt academic goal, which
came from you. Please forgive me for doubting the plans you
ordained for me to be successful. You gave me the strength to
stand on your promises of Philippians 3:14 and 2 Chronicles
20:15b as my dissertation journey took me down winding roads
of challenges and discouragement stemming from a broken

relationship, lack of support, negative criticism, covid 19 pandemic, and loss of my parents. Oh Lord, thanks for your Words of wisdom and support that kept me through this dissertation process successfully. Amen.

On a heightened positive note, in 2011, I started my Ph.D. journey to complement my academic goal. I set out on a positive note, and I did great with the preliminary courses and looked forward to completing the dissertation program in 2014. However, that plan was further from the truth, and unfortunately, due to my failed marriage, I could not complete my doctoral program as planned. I had an ABD (All But Dissertation) experience. The trajectory of my home allowed for me to become a single parent of two girls aged seven and six, which made studying extremely challenging. Also, I had difficulty working with the assigned Chair. We went back and forth on my research topic, and the Chair's feedback was not in alignment with the research topic endeavor. The Chair communicated her concern to me that, in her opinion, I am one of those who did not have the tenacity to complete the doctoral program. I was left powerless and discouraged. Those two factors impeded my doctoral journey, and I threw myself into a self-pity mode for a while, which landed me out of the dissertation program in 2014. I decided, or so I thought, that the Chair was right, and with my personal challenges, it made sense.

Sometime in 2017, my Alumna reached out to offer a partial scholarship for another master's degree in Compliance with a concentration in Health Care Services Administration. I thought it was a brilliant plan and coincided well with my way of life at the time. The duration of the Compliance course was less than two years, so I went ahead with classes. I did well and looked forward to completing the degree. An emergency arose that caused me to travel to Jamaica. I only had one class to complete the degree, and my academic advisor assured me that it was ok to travel since I had only one class remaining. I went to Jamaica on business and came back with great anticipation to complete the master's degree. One month prior to starting class, the university sent out an email stating there was a financial constraint issue that the administrative body was dealing with, but not to worry, they would provide positive feedback soon. I was supposed to resume classes in September 2018, but a month prior to registration, the academic advisor communicated that I would not be able to complete the class or the degree due to a pending bankruptcy of the university. I went into a state of shock and disbelief. I felt disappointed and defeated once again. For three months, I was thrown into a state of questioning God about the failures of my academic dreams.

Soon after, as a courtesy on behalf of the bankrupt university, several universities reached out to assist me in completing the master's degree. During that time, I had several conversations with about 15 universities wanting to accept my credits toward the degree. The process was long and futile, which added to my frustrations of not progressing with my academic dreams. I started to doubt myself and agreed with those individuals who thought I was worthless and did not have what it took to complete my Ph.D. During this time, my older daughter was concerned that I did not complete my Ph.D. I did not realize she noticed and became alarmed. I was thrown into another mindset by my daughters observing me. I could not afford to quit on myself. I fasted and prayed earnestly about my academic dilemma for weeks.

At the beginning of 2019, I received a call from an enrollment specialist at Northcentral University to determine if they had a degree aligned with my classes. Although the exercise was futile, the enrollment specialist was kind and insisted they had a degree that the university could forge for me. Her kind and thoughtful mannerism resonated with me, and we talked on more than one occasion. I saw the opportunity to communicate about my incomplete dissertation program. She revealed that she believed she could assist me in getting back into a Ph.D. program with NCU since it had a Dissertation program formulated for ABD individuals like me. I was overjoyed and decided I wanted to give it a try. The enrollment specialist worked with me in the initial stage to request my transcript from the prior university.

The enrollment process was successful; however, as soon as I was ready to begin the program, I received word from Jamaica that my father had passed suddenly. I was floored with feelings of sadness. I had conflicting feelings about whether this Ph.D. program could be a reality based on the recent loss. I communicated to the academic office that I would not be able to start the doctoral program as planned because I had to travel to Jamaica. I traveled to Jamaica, funeralized my dad, and sadly returned to the United States (my home). I was in a sad state, and I questioned whether I should notify NCU or just quit on myself again. After two weeks of going through emotions, I gathered the strength to reach out to the university. They were elated to hear back from me, and after a final registration process, I was set for my doctoral program. I landed into a wonderful Chair committee and was offered two years to complete the program (2019-2021). I felt enthused to resume my doctoral program, and my children were happy.

I experienced residual feelings from the loss of my father, which impeded my vibrant mindset to commence my doctoral program. I struggled with feelings of loss and confidence for a while, which started to jeopardize my focus on my studies. Eventually, my feelings of the loss of my father subsided, and I became more confident in my academic pursuit. This turning point of a somewhat second chance to complete my dissertation was very clear, and I proceeded. There was constant communication with my Chair, and I soon learned that NCU promulgated strict guidelines for students to complete a partial dissertation in two years. The part that was unclear to me was that I had to dismiss my initial research (I researched the topic and subject for four years). This meant that the four years that I had invested in my research topic and the research content was futile. I had to present a lucrative research topic within the first year. Once again, I thought that this dissertation journey was becoming unsurmountable again. It was another obstacle as I contemplated presenting a research topic in less than half the time as before. As I indicated before, the Chair dissertation committee member was God-sent. We connected on a spiritual and emotional level that spiraled positive energy. Her encouragement was enough assurance for me as I removed the blindfold of doubt from my mind, rolled up my sleeves of mental capacity, and started my research study.

The research went well, and I presented an approved research topic which allowed me to move forward with the groundwork of my research. With hard work that entailed reduced hours of sleep, social life, and even interaction with my children, my dissertation milestones were met over the period leading up to Covid 19 pandemic. It was challenging to work from home and study from home simultaneously. I was spending more time on the job and paying less attention to my research objective and goals. Also, my daughters had to do remote learning, which allowed us to cohabitate in the same space, posing more challenges. I experienced this research setback, but I persisted, planned, and found the time to press on. I persisted through all these obstacles, and the momentum of researching and writing gradually improved and was successful. My Chair communicated that I should be able to complete the program in June 2021.

I was excited and hoped that the completion of my dissertation would be successful. Prior to the Covid 19 pandemic, I was assured that the participants for my research study were on board. Unfortunately, the pandemic shut down that opportunity. I had to conduct a research study with results, and there was no other way. I panicked and became distraught. I went into prayer mode as I reclaimed Philippians 4:13 and 2 Chronicles 20: 15b. A voice within my conscience echoed that I should reach out to the Chair member promptly. We reviewed my dissertation manuscript draft. Based on the problem that I researched and documented, the Chair realized I could reach out to neighboring health care organizations and request their permission to conduct the research study. I conducted the research study; however, my completion date was extended to August 2021.

With more hard work and dedication, I pressed toward my academic goal. The end was in sight. I was overly excited that I would be completing the research study in a matter of months and sweet relief swept over me. I felt a sense of relief as my dissertation manuscript came to fruition, and the Chair and I began to prepare the Oral Defense for the finals. I soon received communication from Jamaica that my mother took ill and was not doing well. My spirit dropped, and I became perplexed. My focus shifted as I communicated with the family about her health and prognosis. I got the news that my mom passed on June 8, 2021. I was devastated and heartbroken as I contemplated traveling to Jamaica to funeralize my mother. I discussed the matter with my Chair, and once more, my program had to be extended, but this would be the final extension. I went to Jamaica, funeralized my mother, and came back in time for my Oral Defense in October 2021, which was successful.

The completion of my dissertation was impacted by challenging issues that tested my spiritual strength and were mentally draining as I struggled and persisted in silence simultaneously. I want to share this story because it can encourage someone in the same predicament and struggles to achieve their life goals. I used my crucibles as stepping stones and, with prayer and supplication, continued the dissertation journey in faith, claiming His promises. You can do that too - trust God to build your resilience in the face of adversities. When you are faced with your crucibles as you embark upon your goals, pray for strength claiming Philippians 4:13 and 2 Chronicles 20:15b. God will give it to you.

Dr. Marine E. Bryan

Dr. Marine E. Bryan has lived in the United States of America for nearly thirty years. She has two teenage daughters who light up her life as a single parent. She holds a Ph.D. in Business Administration with a specialization in Healthcare Administration and currently serves as the Product Benefit Director for a reputable health care service organization in New York. She is an active member in her church, where she currently serves as a Sabbath School Superintendent. She offers volunteering services in Medical Coding and Editing to pass her time. In addition, she finds pleasure in writing, motivational speaking, traveling, reading based on the Bible, cooking, singing, listening to music, exercising, and helping at church. Her greatest joy is engaging in charity by consistently sending barrels with food and clothes to her home district in Jamaica. Her website is currently under construction, but she can be contacted at 347-207-8075.

Jesus Provides Peace and Prosperity in the Place He Plants You
By Jennifer Burton

But seek ye first the kingdom of God, and his righteousness, and
ALL things shall be added unto you.
Matthew 6:33

I am a Mid-Level Manager working for a public Fortune 500 company in the Healthcare Industry, with a little over 20 years of experience in Corporate Internal Audit. As an Internal Auditor, my primary role is to provide reasonable assurance that controls are implemented and working as intended to mitigate risk. These controls are necessary to ensure company objectives are met, financial statements are accurate, and adherence to laws and regulatory requirements. God blessed me with a career that I love. I came to know the Lord at a very young age, and my relationship with Jesus has shown me how great His faithfulness is, and He provides absolute assurance that I am an heir of every promise because He cannot lie. I was born and raised in a small town in Mississippi, and I was fortunate to be raised with a village who always told me of His goodness. As I have matured and built my own relationship with Him, I have been fortunate to taste His goodness for myself.

The promise in God's word in Matthew 6:33 states, "But seek ye first the kingdom of God, and his righteousness, and **ALL** things shall be added unto you." Jesus is Lord of **ALL** and is the source of every promise He made to His heirs. God made these promises by two unchangeable things: an oath and God can't lie. His promises are our treasure and seeking Him, and His righteousness is the **X** that marks the spot where our treasures are stored. Do you believe you can have it **ALL,** or is your belief limited?

In my career as an Internal Auditor, I performed audits to validate if the company was complying with escheatment state laws which require companies to transfer **unclaimed** property from dormant accounts to the state general fund, which takes over record-keeping and returning of lost or forgotten property to owners or their heirs. Examples of unclaimed property are refunds, checking/savings accounts, stocks, uncashed payroll checks, and trust distributions. Dormant is defined as temporarily devoid yet capable of being awakened. There is not a centralized database or one source where all unclaimed property is tracked for every state. The process for reclaiming unclaimed property varies by each state and requires the owner/heir to seek reimbursement by applying with their state at no cost/ free or for a nominal handling fee. So, I ask you, what **unclaimed** promises are lying dormant within you? Unlike unclaimed property, God is the one source where you can claim **ALL** your promises. Unlike unclaimed property, God's promises are unwavering and do not vary because His word is the same yesterday, today, and tomorrow. Similar to unclaimed property, God's salvation is free, and He paid the price. All we need is faith as small as a mustard seed.

My personal testimony of how God provided me peace and prosperity in my career consisted of God revealing and fulfilling these two promises in small doses over the last four years. Now I am able to fully see how He fulfilled peace and prosperity in my life. Over the last four years, these small doses were sometimes hard to swallow but came to me in the following ways: God blessed me with a position that I desired, and when He blessed me, He blessed me like He always had. He opened the door, and all I had to do was just walk through. I did not have to interview or compete with peers for the roles. This was nothing but God's favor. I held that position for a little over a year, and then I had to deal with the hurt and rejection of losing the position due to an acquisition and changes in the department structure and roles. This was when God delivered my first small dose. He told me that I had to be grateful for the doors He opened as well as the doors that He shut. I didn't realize that my season had changed, and the peace that I had previously in the role would no longer be there under new management. Normally when you see businesses under new management, you expect things to be better, but that was not the case in my situation.

Through the hurt and rejection that I felt during this time, my flesh was bruised, and I did things out of the flesh. I started to look for opportunities outside of the company and roles in other departments. The rejection that I was receiving fueled my self-doubt. This was when God delivered my second dose. He told me that I had to remember who I was, whose I was, and that I did not need to be affirmed by man. Even though it was hard to stay in the department, I remembered that He said obedience is better than sacrifice. I had to fix my attitude, which allowed my peace to come back, but it also was where He was going to prosper me. God opened up the windows and poured out blessings to me that I did not have room to receive. He allowed me to prosper greatly. In this phase, He gave me a double dose of peace and prosperity. He also began to reveal why He shut that door. He showed me that the amount of stress and the hours the person working in that role was not what He had for me. Jesus loves us enough that He saves us from ourselves sometimes. We only have a limited amount of visibility, but God sees and knows all.

Then Covid-19 hit, and God allowed me to prosper because this company and job that I was so ready to leave gave me the flexibility that I needed to deal with the adversity and challenges some of us faced with social injustice and uncertainty in the new normal. The wonderful thing about God is He knows what is to come, and He was protecting His children and me. As noted, it was another dose of prosperity, but it was the beginning of Him preparing me for my redirection. Covid allowed me to rethink what was truly important and refocus on a purpose-driven life. All the deaths reminded me that life was short. During this time, He was beginning to prepare a table for me, and that consisted of the yearning to get back in my word, and I participated in a ten-week Bible study on the book of Hebrews in which the theme was Jesus is Better. During this study, I was reminded that Jesus is Lord of all, and He is Superior.

Within a year, the same role I lost became available, and it was sitting on the table. It looked scrumptious, and I was eating with my eyes. I was shocked that the role became vacant so quickly. At first, there was a part of me that was a little excited about the opportunity. There was another side of me that was uninterested. God gently whispered to me that what I have for you is better. When God spoke those words to me, it was a peace that transcended all my understanding, and I did not have a clue what the better was and when it would come to pass. Because of this, I did not apply for the role. A lot of my colleagues were shocked and inquired why I didn't apply for the job. I stopped dead in my tracks and couldn't do anything but give God praise because He is worthy.

Lastly, after a week of not applying for the role and being at peace, I was asked if I would be interested in being a co-author to write a chapter in this book. Jesus had given me the desire a few years ago to write, but I was never clear on what it would be about and had no clue where to start. He has allowed this to come to pass, and He has given me what I needed to write about and the resources. And so, I end with my letter to God as one of praise and thanksgiving to him for giving me everything that I needed during this trial.

Father, I thank you and praise you for loving me unconditionally, forgiving me for every sin that I committed, and providing me grace and mercy even when I was not deserving. God, I know that you will give me everything I need to run this race as I seek you. Lord, continue to give me the peace quoted in John 14:27, "Peace I leave with you; my peace I give you. I do not give to you as the world gives. Do not let your hearts be troubled and do not be afraid". Lord, continue to give me prosperity in all areas of my life, which include my relationships, spirituality, health, and career. The word says in Proverbs 21:21, "Whoever pursues righteousness and love finds life, prosperity, and honor." These scriptures correlate to the promise I am standing on in Matthew 6:33, "But seek ye first the kingdom of God, and his righteousness, and **ALL** things shall be added unto you." I know in you I can have it **ALL** according to your will for my life. I know that in everything, there is a time and season in which things will come to pass. Ecclesiastes 3:1:8 states, "for everything there is a season, A time for every activity under heaven. A time to be born and a time to die. A time to plant and a time to harvest". I was able to harvest peace and prosperity. I thank you for giving me peace and prospering me that I am not bound, and I am free to claim every promise you have for me and generations to come. Thank you for using me to encourage others and remind them to persevere and claim every promise you have for their lives.

This peace and prosperity have allowed me to Reclaim What's Mine!!!!

Jennifer Burton

Jennifer Burton was born and raised in Belzoni, MS, and currently resides in Georgia with her husband of 14 years and one son, who is her pride and joy. She received her bachelor's degree in Accounting from the Historically Black College (HBCU), Mississippi Valley State University, and later received her M.B.A. from Strayer University. She has over 20 years of Internal Audit experience working in Fortune 500 companies in the manufacturing and healthcare industry. She is a Certified Internal Auditor (CIA) and is a Mid-Level Manager. She was brought up with parents, older siblings, and a village of family and church family who always instilled the importance of believing in Jesus and having faith. She has always been active in church and has served in various ministries and leadership roles. Prior to the pandemic, she served in the Children's Ministry and was part of the Stephen Ministry that provides one-on-one care to individuals by walking alongside them when they are hurt or going through a trial or tribulation, so they never feel they have to endure it alone. This is her first time co-authoring a book, and she is honored that God has blessed her with the opportunity to share her testimony of how God has provided peace and prosperity in the places he has planted her. She can be reached via email at jenedwa5@gmail.com.

Authority to Activate Your Power
By Diana Byfield

*Today I give you **authority** over nations and kingdoms to uproot and to pull down, to destroy and to overthrow, to build and to plant.*
Jeremiah 1:10 (GNT)

My name is Diana Byfield. I am the CEO of Purpose Powerhouse LLC and Founder of Sweating with Purpose. I am the mother of one beautiful and intelligent daughter, Dynaijah Armoni. I can say that now that I know why I went through half of the things I encountered. God never left my side, whether I knew of it or not. I had moments in my life when I was angry at God. Nevertheless, He was there through it all, covering me, comforting me, and strengthening me, even when I did not feel it or see it. I know for sure His purpose was greater than my own will and plans.

When I said "Yes" to God's purpose, I did not sign up for the trials and tribulations that came along with it. CCHHILLEEE! But those storms made me more aware of the gifts, skills, and power that God stored in me. Many of us have not stepped into our true divine power when we believe and receive the Son, the Father, and the Holy Spirit. Some people say it's their gut feeling or intuition; however, the Holy Spirit is there to lead us daily, guide us, and stretch us into becoming who God intended us to be.

In the summer of 2015, I was working for DressBarn in New York City. I was in the leadership role as an assistant operations manager. Customer service was my best skill because I am a people person. One day a client walked into the store, and it was my first time meeting this woman. She was African American

31

with light brown skin, and her hair was dark brown in a short pixie cut. She resembled Judge Lynn Toler. The woman was very polite. She came in looking for new items, but while she was in the store, she stopped the store manager and approached her. I noticed she was prophesying to her. I minded my business and kept on working to serve the other clients in the store.

I ended up in the dressing room collecting the clothes that customers had left. The woman of God, yeah, that Prophetess, came right in. She looked at me; I greeted her, then she said, "Can I speak what the Spirit of the Lord wants to say to you?" I wasn't sure what she would say, but I told the Prophetess, "Yes, you may." She started telling me about my past experiences, the things that were done to me, the things I got myself into, and even what I was going through at that moment.

God sent this woman. I couldn't stop my tears from rolling down my face. The Spirit of the Lord spoke through that woman and said, "All that happened in your life was purposed. Many women will follow you because your story is powerful and will touch their minds, hearts, and lives. Your past life stank like dung but when God fixes you up, makes your crooked path straight, you are going to have a sweet fresh aroma in his nostrils."

She continued, "I see women all around you. When you get home, write PURPOSE on your walls. PURPOSE. PURPOSE. PURPOSE!" Then she stopped as if she had seen a quick vision and said in a quiet, still voice, "Your name is Purpose. God called you Purpose." At that time, I was fighting myself to become the person God had called me to be. I was going to church but still had one foot out serving the world. My past of molestation, leaving home at the age of 16, having a miscarriage, being drugged up, raped, and conceiving a child was still haunting me. I became a teen mom, experienced homosexuality, prostitution, anger issues, fighting females and males, going to jail, suicide, depression, and homelessness. I had experienced mental, verbal, physical, sexual, and spiritual abuse. The Promise was that it would **ALL** turn out for good to help others but, more so, women.

Authority is to give power or the right to give orders and to make decisions. Jeremiah 1:10 (NIV) says, **"GOD APPOINTED JEREMIAH."** When the Prophetess spoke into my life, I wasn't ready to act upon what she said about me. I did not believe in myself. I did not surrender to God fully and wholeheartedly. In December of that year, I attempted to go out with friends to a Brooklyn Fete Party. I told God this was my last party, and I would give my life to Him fully. I made up my mind. I was going to this party. So many things went wrong that night, but I was persistent. We reached the location around 2 AM. The line was long, and we were waiting to go in. As soon as we got close to the front door, the Fire Department came and went into the building. About 30 minutes later, the Fire Marshals came out and yelled to all who were waiting in line, "THE BUILDING IS OVER ITS CAPACITY OF PEOPLE THAT'S IN THERE, EVERYONE HAS TO GO HOME!" When God appoints you for His will, He will stop your plans because a promise needs to be fulfilled.

I knew in my heart I wanted to stop rehearsing the same cycle every year, working to make ends meet, to rob Peter to pay Paul. I was constantly involved in unequally yoked relationships with men, hanging around people that did not want to grow, but I wanted more. I wanted to see this better version of Diana. I wanted to see this Promise that God had for me. When God calls, chooses, and appoints you, that is just the beginning of His word and His Promise. You must be ready to be stretched, disciplined, be teachable, and surrender to His will and plans for your life. You will get wisdom, knowledge, and understanding when you start maturing and growing in His Holiness and Righteousness.

To walk into the will of God, you walk in the **authority** of His purpose. Jeremiah 1:9 says, **THE LORD REACHED OUT HIS HAND AND TOUCHED MY MOUTH AND SAID TO ME (Jeremiah), "I HAVE PUT MY WORDS IN YOUR MOUTH."** This aligns with having the authority to activate the power that is gifted in you. I had to know thyself of what God said about me. It's like you must love and study yourself as you study the word of God. Believe in His word, take yourself and your future seriously. Your mindset must rise if you receive the wisdom of the Lord. God places the right words to uplift you in your journey, give you power and authority to speak life over yourself daily.

Ask yourself…

Do you believe in the promise that God has for you? Do you believe in His word? Do you believe you are able to see your Promise(s)? Are you willing to initiate to get to the Promise? Are you speaking in His Authority to activate your power and to see it through to possess your promise(s) to be fulfilled?

I had to believe in God's word, His promise, and myself. My church always held Consecration on the first Sunday of the month. On the first Sunday in October 2019, we had a special speaker, and he was a prophet. As the Holy Spirit led the man of God, he called me out during his sermon about THE YEAR OF PEY (per the Jewish Calendar year; it was the year of mouth, what you shall speak it shall manifest). The man of God said, "There is a not-for-profit organization spirit inside of you, and the Spirit of the Lord wants me to remind you that he is getting you ready for where you are about to go in the next five years. There is a business plan inside of you, and it has to grow." The prophet went on and said, "Don't (seven times)" then paused and continued, "I hear the Lord saying the word DON'T! Don't allow yourself to stop yourself because of what you think you don't have!"

The Prophet told me that I needed to **prophesy over myself** that day and go forward to do it because **I believe it**. This is where my faith had to level up. By October 23, 2019, I received a letter that I was let go of by my job, a not-for-profit organization. Their funding from the city of New York under HRA was being cut. I didn't see it coming that suddenly, but I was well prepared in my spirit. The next morning, I went into prayer, seeking a word from God. The Spirit of the Lord led me to Isaiah 43:19 - "FOR I AM ABOUT TO DO SOMETHING NEW. SEE, I HAVE ALREADY

BEGUN! DO YOU NOT SEE IT? I WILL MAKE A PATHWAY THROUGH THE WILDERNESS. I WILL CREATE RIVERS IN THE DESERT." I knew that was directly from God telling me His hands are in this. He was reassuring me not to doubt, to stand firm in faith, and trust Him.

This faith walk is not easy, but God is a never-failing God. He is more faithful to us than we are to Him. As the word says,

"So shall my word be that goes out from my mouth; it shall accomplish that which I purpose and shall succeed in the thing for which I sent it."
Isaiah 55:11

You have the authority and willpower to see your promise come to fruition. Jeremiah 1:10 stated God had given Jeremiah authority and appointed Him over nations and kingdoms. Jeremiah had the ability to root out, pulldown, destroy, throw down, build, and plant. I decided to walk by faith, believe in myself, and most importantly, speak, affirm, and prophecy God's word. With the authority God has given us, we are able to:

- Root out things in our lives
- Pull down thoughts that are not of God
- Destroy or put an end to what is not serving our purpose(s)
- Throw down what comes against us
- Build what God has given us in our hands
- Plant the seeds of joy, happiness, wealth, and abundance within our families, communities, organizations, and the world

You have the power within you to accomplish the task at hand. Can you see it now?

As 2 Timothy 1:7 says, "God did not give us the spirit of fear, but of **power**, and of love, and of a sound mind (His peace).

God has given you the authority to activate the power that He has given you.

How can you activate the power?

Speaking and holding onto His word and His Spirit will activate your confidence, hope, determination, resilience, and purpose. If God leads you to your promise, you are planted in purpose and humility. I believe every believer of Christ should be able to stand firm in God's authority to activate their power to do all things through Christ, to accomplish what you are led to do, and see the promise of what the Lord told you. You have the power to shift things, build, pull down, and root out what comes in your way. Start planting your seeds, work diligently, have faith, speak, affirm God's word, and watch it manifest.

Dear Father,

I see the purpose in your prophecies, visions and hearing your voice to be led to the promise. Thank you for never leaving me when I doubted and didn't believe in you or myself. I literally see it all coming together as you spoke. Looking back, I can say I came a long way. You made something out of nothing. You covered my daughter and me. You gave me a reason to live when I was ready to give up ten years ago. There was a purpose to live, uplift, encourage, and empower. Daddy, you helped me release so I could help those connected to me do the same. You helped me pull down and root out my self-sabotaging mindset. You made me see my worth. I will build your kingdom to prosper for your Glory. Thank you for loving me for who I am. With flaws and all, you still call me your daughter. Thank you for including me in the vision of your promise. I thank you for giving me the authority to activate the power within.

Love you always,
Diana Byfield as "Purpose"

Diana Byfield

Diana Byfield was born in Harbor View, Kingston Jamaica. She is a single mother of one daughter, Dynaijah Armoni. Ms. Byfield is CEO of Purpose Powerhouse L.L.C. and Founder of Sweating with Purpose. She was awarded and honored as Purpose Driven in her community. She was also given an Official Statement for Her Excellency by the State of Connecticut in 2021. She made a special appearance on Rolling Out Magazine, Been Worthy, and various blogs. She was also featured on The Chundria Show (YouTube Influencer) and CT Channel 12 News.

Ms. Byfield is a Certified Wellness Purpose Coach as well in success and happiness. Purpose Powerhouse focuses on helping women to overcome depression and anxiety to prosper with their life, mind, body, and spirit. Created and birthed out of Diana's past pain, abuses, low self-esteem, and depression. Sweating with Purpose is a program that covers wellness and dance fitness. She will soon launch an activewear collection for women to feel, wear, and activate their power. Her life coaching sessions and her goal to build an afro-beats, Caribbean, and hip-hop/inspiration-infused dance fitness studio with meditation classes would help other women see themselves as a Purpose Powerhouse!

Do not be deceived by the evidence!
By Kirsha Campbell

For God hath not given us the spirit of fear; but of power, and of love, and of a sound mind
2 Timothy 1:7 (KJV)

"Kirsha, you know I don't like you," my classmate in primary school calmly said. Those words stung, especially since she provided no reason not to like me. I can't recall hearing a reason; however, I recall those words quite clearly decades after they were said to me.

I stood waiting to be picked on, uncomfortable as always. Name after name was called, but my name was called last as usual. I knew they didn't mean any harm. After all, they were my friends. We were in Physical Education Class, and as usual, I was the last one to be selected to be on a team.

Those are two of the many early memories I have of being rejected by friends, family, or even strangers. Rejection appears in your life in so many ways leaving many scars, crippling you with fear and uncertainty. The rejection led me not to claim many promises from my Daddy (Daddy God!).

"They will laugh at me."

"I will always be a misfit."

"No one will want to spend time with me."

"I am not fun enough."

"I have nothing of value to add."

"I will sound silly; furthermore, they will not understand me."

"If only I wasn't so fat."

Those are just some of the internal dialogues I have had over the years. The spirit of rejection became a part of my life very early. It led me to be afraid to try new things, take risks, be honest about my feelings, and most importantly to tap into the power, love, and sound mind that God gave me. And the spirit of rejection in my life soon had a partner - the spirit of fear. I forgot that God had gifted me with power, love, and a sound mind. So, I NEVER opened the gift until recently when I embraced the scripture; He *is able to do abundantly exceedingly more than you can ask or imagine* (Ephesians 3:20 paraphrased). As I reflect, I talk to my Daddy - Daddy God.

Dear Daddy,

I just finished my second round of paid training for international executives in countries outside of my home country. Daddy, I reflect in awe that this was actually me.

"Little me."

Little me who used to be shy and afraid to speak in board meetings, groups, or around people in general. I would never say a word most of the time unless someone asked me a question.

Little me who would ever so often question my worth or the value I offered to others.

Daddy, they even gave me amazing reviews and feedback. I am beaming and giving you all the praise and glory. The reviews were REALLY spectacular. Were they really about me?

Daddy, what if I had kept being afraid and wondering if I would be rejected? How different would the trajectory be for those companies, their employees, clients, and the world?

Thank you, Daddy. Each day I realize my fear and rejection could have stopped me from taking new and different steps that would impact myself and those you have divinely put in my path in various ways and at different times. What if I never tried again? What if I allowed my failures and disappointments to cripple my efforts to try again?

I think of my very first client when I started my business; their revenue has grown over 300% in under four years. Yet, I doubted myself so many times, wondering if I could actually do what I claimed I could. I think of the impact not only on my clients but the rippling effect on their employees, teams, families, and the world at large. I am so thankful I trumped my fear and started this journey to support business owners, CEOs, companies, and organizations.

Daddy, I am beyond grateful that you continue to carry me and give me strength, even when I think I can't take another step. However, I must be honest, Daddy. I am not grateful for the pain and hurt. Nope. No way. I am grateful for the lessons learned and the ones I am yet to learn. I have grown in so many ways, Daddy. I look in awe that this is really me!

When I started this entrepreneurial journey, it was lonely, Daddy. I was alone with my boys most of the time, and they were about two years old. I remember the sleepless nights, the times I cried, the confusion about the next step, the disappointment when it didn't grow as I thought it would, and the many times I thought of giving up.

Surgeries and developmental delays are some of what we had to maneuver in the early years of my little boys. Some moments were very frightening and even unpredictable. I claimed many promises over my little ones. Today, I realize that they were truly handpicked and a priceless gift from you, Daddy. I stand in awe of the promises you unfold in your perfect time.

I am thankful that I finally learned it is ok to integrate the moving parts of my life - family, work, volunteer and realize it will be a continuous improvement. It is also ok not to be ashamed that I have chosen to put my little ones first. You know, Daddy, the times I felt embarrassed when they said hi while I was in a meeting with a client or the times I experienced peer pressure about their development. Today, I chose to be thankful for it all and embrace how much my little ones continue to teach me daily, Daddy. But can I be honest, Daddy? The suffering is no fun. I admit I would prefer to skip the suffering and go straight to the lesson, kind of like when I prefer to go straight to having dessert before the meal. Who says dessert has to always be last, right?

And after you have suffered a little while, the God of all grace, who has called you to his eternal glory in Christ, will himself restore, confirm, strengthen, and establish you.
1 Peter 5:10

Daddy, thank you also for blessing me with my first international speaking/training appointment – another "is this really me, God" moment. Moments like that makes me reflect on the scriptures, *I will restore to you the years (*Joel 2:25-26) and *For I will restore health to you, and your wounds I will heal, declares the LORD (*Jeremiah 30:17).

Daddy, do you remember the mixed emotions I felt when I was moving to Canada? I was excited and scared, plus so many other emotions. Right, Daddy? I had so much to learn – new cultures, new experiences, new me - I continue to learn each day, of course. I was afraid to speak, and I kept thinking whatever I said would be of no great value and would be rejected. Yet today, I am an international speaker.

Daddy, I know I've dwelt on past hurt and allowed it to stand in my way. When I was treated differently and "not nice" because of my accent or my home country, that hurt BIG TIME; again, it led me to question my worth and value as a person. The truth is hurt, pain, and rejection are real, but I also know that healing and growth are, too. And I want my reader to understand that as well.

Daddy, I've allowed my past to filter into my business endeavors as well. I felt broken when a prospective sale was not closed, and I didn't get the client. I felt broken when my pitch to Entrepreneur

Magazine was rejected. I still feel broken and disappointed when my goals, both personal and professional, were not met.

But my God, I am thankful that I continue to rely on your promises. Years ago, you told me in a dream that it would be ok. Life will be ok one day. It will fall into place. The dust will settle the best way – your way. You were so right, Daddy.

Today, I am a writer for Entrepreneur magazine. I now do live trainings for corporations. I have a segment on a local TV station. I am now featured on podcasts and other forms of media. I am learning how to grow into a better woman and mother to my little ones even while I build and grow professionally. I am learning to be thankful daily.

The twists, turns, and disappointments have led me to know myself more and be willing to change in areas that make me a better person. I have seen you literally carry me, Daddy, when I could not take another step on my own. I had to let go of so much to allow you to work in my life, Daddy.

Daddy, do you remember Moses? He was afraid, and you gave him words

Now go! I will help you as you speak, and I will teach you what to say.
Exodus 4 12

Daddy, like Moses, I know you have more work for me to do. I have growth to step into; there are better versions of me to be actualized. Change and growth are hard, Daddy, very hard. It will be worth it, though. I am learning to let go of old habits to start new ones. I am learning to admit my shortcomings and grow from them. I am starting to lean into your truth more, Daddy, even when the "evidence" tells me otherwise. I have recently been embracing your words, even more, Daddy:

For God hath not given us the spirit of fear; but of power, and of love, and of a sound mind
2 Timothy 1:7 (KJV)

43

I don't need to be afraid anymore. I know things will turn around in your time and in your way. I am committed to reaching the finish line with you, Daddy. No longer am I shrinking back. No more being afraid of failure or rejection, Daddy. No more giving up on the first no or even the second. Daddy, I believe it will come to pass. I do not doubt you anymore. I am trusting you fully, Daddy. It is time to let go of my feelings and rely on your facts, Daddy. I know you love me unconditionally, and my business and life are redemptions for my bloodline. I am not giving up on the dreams; you are my ultimate redeemer, Daddy. Standing alone is never easy, but standing for you and with you, Daddy, is worth it.

I step out on faith and allow you to take me to my promise(s). I will be loyal to the promise and be postured for my breakthrough. I repent of my unbelief, trying my own plans and going when you said to wait or waiting when you said to go. I am trusting all your words that you have given, Daddy. I know that you will release all held-up promises, Daddy. I trust in your instructions and strategy. I am willing to act when you speak; no longer will I hear your voice and not move, Daddy. No more tantrums, Daddy. No more fussing when I realize I can't do it all on my own. Change my attitude, Daddy, please. I am willing to be different with you. I trust you and know you care about the details in my life - what I wear, eat, how I feel, and so much more. No longer will I want the promise and not be willing to be obedient, Daddy. I will check my posture and be willing to wait, Daddy. Your promises are true and worth waiting for.

Daddy, I am claiming all my unclaimed promises and thanking you for when they will manifest. Rejuvenate my faith and cancel doubt, despite all my disappointments. Let me not keep rehashing the past. Daddy, I know the best is yet to come. This is not even your best life for me yet. I will continue to wait with expectancy and get excited each day. Yes, Daddy, even when there are sad days or disappointing times, I will not remain there, but keep pushing along with you!

Your Daughter,
Kirsha

For I know the plans I have for you," declares the LORD, "plans to prosper you and not to harm you, plans to give you hope and a future.
Jeremiah 29:11

What if I fall, Oh my darling what if you fly?
Winnie the Pooh

Whenever I say goodbye to fear and rejection, it is critical to realize saying goodbye doesn't mean that I am pretending that I am not feeling fear or rejection. After all, I still do from time to time. It means I have learned to acknowledge that I am feeling rejection and fear at a particular moment, and that is ok.

Through prayer, I assess why and listen to God or talk to a trusted person. I take steps to replace rejection and fear with promises from GOD.

We destroy arguments and every lofty opinion raised against the knowledge of God and take every thought captive to obey Christ
2 Corinthians 10:5 ESV

Sometimes It takes reading and re-reading the promises and claiming them, despite not seeing any signs of fruition or not "feeling or believing" the promises at that point in time.

You can replace rejection and fear with promises from GOD, too.

The days when you don't "feel" like doing XYZ, acknowledge those feelings, then assess what if I stop, what will be my result, or what if I keep going, what will be my reward? Most times, after my tantrums or rebellion, I know I must keep going. There is too much to gain to lose. I know the same is true for you too.

My friend and sister, God is not finished with you or me yet. Isn't that exciting? Doesn't that give you hope to try one more time, to take that risk, or even to relax knowing He has got your back? What promise do you need to claim or reclaim from God today?

Being confident of this very thing, that he which hath begun a good work in you will perform it until the day of Jesus Christ
Philippians 1:6

Where there is no vision... the people perish
Proverbs 29:18

I will instruct thee and teach you the way you should go
Psalm 32:8

The Next Steps
- What can you be thankful for at this moment?

- What promises have God already delivered in your life?

- Temperature check—how are you feeling at this moment? Do you need to vent to God, scream, cry, etc.? IT IS OK – DO IT.

- What promises by God can you claim at this moment?

- Be still and listen – allow God to tell you the next steps.

- Smile, breathe; it will be OK.

Kirsha Campbell

Kirsha Campbell is a twin mom to amazing little boys who keep her learning and re-learning. They enjoy spending time outdoors in nature, going on hikes, and taking walks. As a CPA, CMA, she is passionate about helping SMEs become equipped with the tools and strategies needed to survive in business—especially in times of crisis—as well as moving them from profits to cash flow by using strategic financial systems. Her passion for details and continuous improvement and growth has led her to help different businesses with diverse backgrounds and in different industries improve cash flow, save on costs, increase value, reduce waste, revamp strategy, and more!

She has learned the importance of listening to business owners, understanding their pain points and issues—without judging—and working together to implement customized, creative, and effective solutions and strategies to result in more cash flowing into their businesses. More than simply educating you as the business owner, we work together to look beyond the numbers to tap into the heart of your business—the processes, the plans, the goals, what is working, what is not working, and what can be improved. She transitioned from the corporate world after embracing the vision to support business owners.

She enjoys reading and believes in volunteering and community involvement, and as to that end, she will often be found serving in some way in any community she resides in.

God Is Always With Me, Giving Me The Strength To Go On
By Sabrina N. Clarke

Fear thou not; for I am with thee: be not dismayed; for I am thy GOD: I will strengthen thee; yea, I will help thee; yea, I will uphold thee; with the right hand of my righteousness.
Isaiah 41:10

This scripture means so much to me, and it has kept me strong in faith, trusting and believing in GOD's words. Whenever I go through a situation in my life journey, I remember GOD's words not to be afraid because HE is always with me, strengthening me and holding me as I ride out the storm. And so, I pray…

Good morning, my Father and my Maker. I want to say thank YOU for a new day, thank YOU that YOUR compassion is renewed every morning. Great is YOUR faithfulness and YOUR steadfast love, O LORD! I don't know what will happen today or how much I will get done, but YOU do so; I give this day to YOU. Keep me, my family, and my friends safe at all times, in the mighty, mighty name of JESUS. O LORD, LORD of manifestation, I thank YOU that YOU will cause every good word spoken over my life to come to pass, to receive divine manifestation of wealth, prosperity, and open doors. GOD, every promise YOU spoke over my life, let it be manifested in my life. I declare that YOUR word, O' LORD, will destroy any and every weapon trying to delay my divine manifestation. In the name of JESUS, I command every weapon delaying the manifestation of my miracles to be destroyed. I speak with power and authority that every enemy sent to stop the manifestation of my miracles and blessings will be consumed by the fire of GOD, in the mighty, mighty name of JESUS.O GOD, set a hedge of protection around my life. Release me from every trap set before me and protect me from the hands of the wicked. O' LORD, I thank YOU for protecting and preserving me. Preserve me and protect me from the enemy, familiar spirits, any and all wickedness. I speak total protection over my life according to YOUR word in Psalm 91. I declare with power and authority that I shall dwell in the secret place of the Most High and abide under the shadow of the Almighty, in the name of JESUS. AMEN and AMEN.

I wanted to start with a prayer to show my gratitude to YOU, as I do every morning. This is your favorite daughter Sabrina Clarke. YOU have been so good to me that I wake up every morning feeling ANOINTEDLY BLESSED AND HIGHLY FAVORED; despite what's going on with my feelings, I just can't help it. All honor and glory belong to YOU, LORD. YOU have done so much for me that I cannot tell it all, but I will start with being laid off from my 18-year job in 2009. I was in the tourism industry working in the housekeeping department, and the world was in a recession. The hotel decided they had to release some of the staff. I never told my sister about my decision to talk with the department head because the company employed families, and I knew they would let go a mother, daughter, or sister. Since my husband and I had already invested in a hardware store with my husband's brother and his wife, I told them to let me be the one to be laid off. My husband agreed with me and told me I have been working for 18 years, and I can take this time to relax. He said he could handle this. I told him to let me know if things get unbearable and I would get another job. Through YOUR grace and mercy, we are now in 2021, and he is still holding the family together. There were times when things got hard, but YOU always make things better.

Once we started to build some townhouses and that ate into our savings. We were living paycheck to paycheck, but GOD, you showed up again, and we were able to move out of our apartment and into one of the townhouses. After selling the townhouses, we built a beautiful home, debt-free, with no mortgage, and only paying utilities. I know only YOU, LORD, could have taken us through the journey of moving out of our parent's home into our apartment to our own townhouse then into a debt-free home. Without YOU, none of this would have been possible.

I joined a company called Ardysslife, and they stand on their motto of Faith Family Lifestyle and Legacy. I joined to get the nutritional products they offered to help me with my high cholesterol. At the time, I was diagnosed with borderline hypertension. After being on the Ardysslife products for two weeks, my cholesterol level was lower, and I lost ten pounds. I was overweight for my height of five feet three inches and weighed 172 pounds. From then on, I never had cholesterol issues again because I have remained on the products since 2013. GOD said the plants are for the healing of the land. There HE was showing up again in my life.

I needed a way to get rid of the cholesterol issue without taking the medication. My doctor had prescribed Crestor, and I said I was not going to fill it. GOD showed up with my cousin, who introduced me to the Ardysslife all-natural products. Now, I'm free from the medication and free from high cholesterol. After seeing the results myself, I decided to go into the business side and help families thrive. I was met with many roadblocks, speed bumps, and stop signs, but I kept the faith and never gave up. I would always hear HIM say to me, "continue to fight; there are people who need these products." I was able to assist so many people with weight loss, health ailments, and financial gain. If it wasn't for GOD's grace and mercy, I would have given up. There was a lady diagnosed with stage four cancer, and she is now cancer-free from using the Ardyss products. Another is coming back to normalcy after having two strokes from high blood pressure after giving birth. I am also working with a neighbor who has diabetes and gave me a report that in all her years of being diagnosed with diabetes, she has never seen the type of numbers she's seeing now while losing 15 pounds in two and a half weeks of being on the Ardysslife products. GOD, I see you in every way helping me get through.

You have helped my family and me through the Covid-19 pandemic. I have been elevated to a new rank in the company while the world is partially shut down, and it's all because of your grace and mercy. I love You more than anything. On the way home from the airport on a holiday trip with her friends, my daughter was in a car accident. I was home waiting for her to call and say she was at the airport but received a call saying she was in an accident and at the hospital. That was a time when I needed you, and you showed up. Your grace and mercy brought me through because I could not get to her until the next day, and it was the longest Monday night in my life. I got a flight out on Tuesday morning, and all I packed were my Ardysslife products. I went to the hospital to see her and everyone that had been hurt in the accident. My daughter told me she couldn't go to the restroom since the day before, and I told her that when she finished drinking these Ardysslife products, she should. And she did soon after she ate and drank the Ardysslife juice I mixed. She asked her daddy and me to help her get us to use the restroom. She asked when our return flight was. I told her Thursday evening. She asked if we would leave her, and I said, no, we all are leaving together. You will be discharged on Thursday. I found out about her medication, and one of them was Percocet. She was concerned because it's an addictive drug and told her not to take any more of it. I gave her the Ardysslife products three times a day, and she was discharged on Thursday afternoon. She had a broken collarbone, three broken ribs, a cracked hairline in her chest, and lost a toenail that they said would take a year to grow back. We all left that Thursday evening on a flight home by GOD's grace and mercy, and I nursed her back to health with the Ardysslife products. I never gave her any pain medication because the Ardysslife products are made from GOD's fruits and vegetables. There HE goes showing up again, never leaving me nor forsaking me, taking away all my fears, giving me the strength to give my daughter the strength to go on. The toenail they said would take a year to grow back took about five months. By the grace of GOD, my daughter is healed and living a normal life with no issues.

My son was also in an accident that flipped the car over, and he crawled out without a scratch on his body, had no broken bones, and was taken to the hospital just for a checkup. When I reached the accident scene and saw the car, he was sitting on the ground next to a wall. I realized he had no scratches or bruises and wasn't hurt, just in shock; I couldn't help but cry out to GOD, thanking HIM for HIS mercy, grace, guidance, and protection. My GOD is always with my family and me. The power of prayer is still working. The weapons may form, but they won't prosper. I will continue to keep my faith strong, leaning on the promises of GOD, my savior. I will not fear but believe that HE is with me every day, everywhere, and in everything. I will not be dismayed because HE is my GOD who will strengthen me, help me, and uphold me with HIS right hand of HIS righteousness.

I want to tell you, my reader, that if GOD brought you to it, HE will bring you through it. You will be tested. You will be tried with stop signs, speed bumps, and potholes along life's journey. Sometimes you may feel like you can't take it anymore but know that GOD is right there with you. If that's how you felt yesterday, and you woke up this morning, that should tell you GOD isn't done with you yet. Hold on to the promises through GOD's words and PUSH (Pray Until Something Happens).

Sabrina N. Clarke

Sabrina Clarke was born January 20, 1972, to her proud parents Godfrey and Louise Murphy (deceased), in the beautiful island of Nassau, Bahamas. She is married to Clayton Clarke and was gifted with two beautiful children, Clayton and Claytina, born on the same day, seven years apart. She started school at the Centerville Primary School and attended the Donald Davis Junior High and R.M. Bailey Senior High School.

She worked at the Comfort Suites Hotel on Paradise Island, New Providence, Bahamas, for 18 years from 1991 to 2009. During that time, she was certified in many different positions in the tourism industry as she made the decision to take every course and training the hotel offered. Some of the certifications and honors received are:

- Certificate of merit and registered as a Bahama host
- Certified in Caribbean Regional Hotel Delivers
- Dream Program and Pathway To Customers Delight Program
- Certified by the Carib Cert, Professional Certification for Housekeeping Supervisors
- Honored by American Express and the Caribbean Hotel Association

- Diploma in Caribbean Hospitality Training Institute Train the Trainer Seminar

She is also an Ardysslife Distributor at the Manager B level and has received The Qualify Performer Award, a Leaderships Award from Ardysslife Training University.

Your Faith Heals
By Khaydeann Dolphy

"And he said unto them, This kind can come forth by nothing, but by prayer and fasting."
Mark 9:29

I was healed on a mountain top in the Catskills when I dared God to prove Himself to me. I was desperate, and I dare say, I was bold. I needed God to heal me. I am 30 years old and bleeding to death. There was nowhere I could go, and no one I could turn to but God. I have served the Lord in every church I've had my membership in. I have served in almost every capacity, sang in every youth or mass choir, led the praise team, assisted in prayer ministry, been an assistant to my mother in women's ministry, and yet, here I was, bleeding each and every day since I was 13 years old. I felt crazy, dirty, unloved, angry, but most of all, I felt tired. How is it that I was serving the one, true, and living God, and I can't see my miracle? Where was my breakthrough? I felt so low. Each week I served my church, even throughout the pandemic. Sometimes I was the first to arrive at church and the last to leave, singing in my church and out of state for the conference events, traveling from plane to plane, and ministering state by state to the people of God, but I wanted to give up. However, before giving up, in what felt like the final card in my deck, my last option, I decided to fast and pray—something I had never done before in my life. If I'm honest, it should have been the first thing I did, but I digress. I grasped my Bible and read out loud, "And he said unto them, 'This kind can come forth by nothing, but by prayer and fasting'" (Mark 9:29). Desperation has a sound. It's inaudible.

Fasting and praying was equivalent to a death sentence for me. I cannot be more transparent than that. My 'pet name' from my predominantly Jamaican family is 'Oxtail.' That ought to tell you about my appetite. I remember seeing a child therapist when I was about six years old. I remember sitting in the cold, sterile pediatric office with mismatched cartoon characters from various shows plastered on the wall, in a sad attempt to make children feel more relaxed, while my doctor asked me several questions about how I felt when I ate my meals. I began to excitedly describe the aroma of the spices that accompanied each meal that were my favorite because, if you must know, the spices for curried goat and the spices for brown stew chicken, my dear, are just simply not the same! I delicately explained the impact of the essence of garlic as it permeates my nostrils right before taking a bite. I distinctly recall telling her of the joy of scarfing down a stolen donut and the delight of sneaking away from home to the corner to purchase a bottle of soda, a Jamaican brand called 'Ting' to be exact (as I wasn't allowed sugary drinks). My doctor, point blankly, looked at my mother and told her with a straight face that there was nothing psychologically wrong with me, that I was just greedy and fat. She should've said it louder for the people in the back because, until this day, food still brings me joy. It was food that had to crush the head and bruise the heel of my medical condition that had laid dormant during my childhood. Removing food and submitting myself to God was the ultimate test for me as my body needed to be healed, and I knew that that could come from only God Himself.

At the age of 18, I was graduating from high school, getting ready to go to college, and coping with severe anemia, as I had been bleeding nonstop for at least two years. I truly felt like the woman with the issue of blood (Mark 5: 25-34). With the help of a daughter of the first Elder at the church I attended, I got birth control from a local clinic where she brought me. I have no idea how she knew about that clinic, but birth control was like a band-aid over the staples of an open-heart surgery. I knew it was a temporary fix and that something was truly wrong with me. Fast forward to a decade later, yes, a decade, I finally decided to visit an OBGYN that I could relate to or that I felt saw *me*. As soon as I sat down before her in March 2020, she told me, on sight, that I had an incurable disease known as polycystic ovarian syndrome.

I was shocked by my diagnosis of PCOS. Even more shocking is that I had a Primary Care Physician of another race for almost eight years, at the same office, who had my results of multiple follicles on my ovaries done via ultrasound at least five years prior, but never sent me for further testing or provided a referral for an OB follow up. The first order of business my OB/GYN ordered was to lose 20 pounds and take a medication commonly known as Metformin. I know this medication; people with diabetes take it to control their blood sugar levels. I felt like she was diagnosing me with diabetes and broke down in tears. I resolved to take the medication and regretted the decision. It made me nauseous. I had a headache all day, every day, and I was STILL bleeding. The first question that came to mind was, what's wrong with me? As a woman, you know that some of the issues we are dealing with have been present since our childhood, like mine, for instance. I always knew something was wrong, but I now felt blemished, broken, and not made in the image of God. I became a graduate of Google University at this point and had led myself into a deep depression.

I was now engaged and soon to be married. This diagnosis brought up all my worst fears. The most obvious in my mind was that I might never be a birth mother. I cried like a baby. How could this be my lot in life? I have an aunt who has no children, and I always said I never wanted to be like her. This is simply the truth. I saw in her eyes how not being able to conceive made her feel. I distinctly remember one weekend when she was babysitting her Goddaughter and, at the time, she was a breastfed child. My aunt, 'jokingly,' whipped out her breast to give the baby while she was crying, asking, "Is this what you want?" The then-baby, because she is about 14 months old at this point, looked at her breast as if to say, 'what *is* that?' I saw the look of embarrassment on my aunt's face at the fact that not even a starving, crying child, who is breastfed and should know instinctively what her boob is, rejected her. None of the logical facts like she is not her mother, the child doesn't recognize the scent of her breast or even the fact that she has no breast milk production to offer the child, registered.

What registered, and I saw it, *I caught that moment in her eyes,* the lack within herself. That she was unable to produce food to offer the child, she felt embarrassed. There was also an altercation amongst aunts in my family where another aunt told the said aunt, 'move with your powdered eggs' meaning; her eggs were old and no longer viable like milk that has been dehydrated to the powdered form for preservation. That insult burned deep, as she is the only child of my grandmother that does not have children. That malicious statement created a horrible rift, one that hasn't quite healed if I must be truthful. My Jamaican family has no filter, and often, their words cut deep. I *cannot* imagine them calling me barren, in or out of my presence.

My fiancé and I often speak of having children and would adopt if we were unable to conceive, but the thought of not having life within me broke me like nothing ever has before. That thought was the single most vile, putrid thing ever to be conceived in my mind. I was overcome with fear, depression, pain, sorrow, and heartache for the simple longing I never knew I had but may now never be afforded to me. I was plagued from that moment on; all I saw were baby commercials, pregnant women, and friends and family on my timeline sharing the exciting news of getting pregnant during the pandemic. There are A LOT of pandemic babies. I was so happy and overjoyed for everyone. My belly burned with the thought of never having that opportunity, of sharing my own news of a successful pregnancy.

I wept and cried before the Lord. It was only moaning and groaning, but the Bible says that He interprets them. I had so many things going right in my life but could only focus on what I *thought* was going wrong. I wanted the hormonal peace that came with a regular cycle. Having PCOS is an *emotional* rollercoaster, and I just wanted to feel 'normal.' I have learned that no woman is normal; however, waking up with ridiculous cravings and being a walking emotional rollercoaster is simply not normal.

The diagnosis made me feel like a prisoner in my own body, and the only thing that I could give unto the Lord was prayer and fasting. Many people complain about the pandemic. I understand why. I am a nurse and have worked throughout the pandemic in NYC, the original epicenter. No one understands how heavy a toll the pandemic has taken more than I do. From the death of my patients to colleagues, to seeing doctors who believed only in science and even atheists, having to turn around asking us, nurses, and the CNAs on staff to pray with and for them was powerful. The pandemic also allowed worship from home. One such ministry born in the pandemic is called 'Breaking the Mold Ministry' from the mind of Pastor Devonte Gilchrist, who is currently studying Theology at Andrews University.

As I began to fast and pray, I went through the fire—hunger like never before. I had to download audible books to help me from the very first day. I intended to fast for forty days and forty nights, and I wasn't sure if I would make it. Literally, I thought about food day and night. I started dreaming about food, which was very disturbing. I eat kosher due to being an Adventist, and I was salivating over shrimps and crab legs! These are things I have never eaten a day in my life! Everywhere I turned was another food commercial, so I cut off the cable. On social media, all I saw were ASMR videos of food by Mukbangers, so I removed Instagram and Facebook apps from my iPhone. I was taking drastic measures because I needed drastic results. I was not eating anything, only drinking Poland spring water and Vita coconut water on days I felt like I was passing out. This was a true test, not only of my faith but my willpower. Food was a stronghold on my life, causing me to be sick, and I was determined to break that yoke in Jesus' name.

I was praying three times a day. My neighbors on every side could hear me, and I did not care. I must be delivered. Jesus had to see me through this storm, and I refused to eat until God blessed me. I was tired. I was tired of bleeding, tired of buying sanitary napkins; the clerks at Walgreens knew me and would quickly ring me up with all my feminine care products in tow. My life was not my own. I was always tired - physically, spiritually, and emotionally. Always consciously checking if I have a stain on my pants or skirt, always conscious of the darkened area of my neck, conscious of the hair that grows on my neck, and all my baggage that accompanies PCOS. I needed God to heal me. I was tired of crying. I was tired of my weight fluctuating. I was tired of the chemical burns from using Nair on my neck. I was tired of having to cancel events or finding a replacement for something I had agreed to do simply because I was exhausted from anemia. I live in NYC where everyone is always so busy, and it seems like one cares. I kept singing the hymn 'Does Jesus Care? Oh yes, He cares, I know He cares, his heart is touched with my grief."

While fasting and praying, my manager at work tried to fire me, but she ended up getting fired herself. At the same time, everything that could go wrong did. I developed a lump in my right breast. I had a breakout that covered my entire body. My sister, also a nurse for 15 years, got stuck by a needle from an HIV patient, and ended up with walking pneumonia. On the Fourth of July, my fiancé and I ended up in a church scandal that was not true, but it was the eleventh commandment to some. A scandal at a church we did not even attend. That same night my nephew ended up in a car accident that totaled the car, but miraculously he walked out alive! So, when I tell you everything went wrong, I mean everything. When you begin to fast and pray, prepare yourself! You will experience battles you may have never faced before.

It was during this fast that Breaking the Mold Ministries had their first Mountain Top Retreat in the Catskills. We immediately felt that the glory of the Lord was about to fill that place. We saw saints prophesying; and miracles happened right before my very eyes. I remember standing under the tent during the worship service, overcome with emotions and crying, when I heard the voice of God clearly, "It is finished." I was fasting for a few things, but I felt a change within me when I opened my eyes. It wasn't until two weeks after leaving that mountain that I used the restroom for the first time since I was 18 years old and saw no blood. I screamed Hallelujah so loud that I was overcome with emotions and began sobbing on the toilet. God is great, and He is worthy to be praised. Some things cannot and will not break until we deny our flesh. Then and only then will we see the goodness of the Lord. I can now say, I have tasted and have seen that the Lord is good! You too can have this experience.

Khaydeann Dolphy

Khaydeann Dolphy is a nurse residing in New York City who loves the Lord. As an avid reader, her passion for books led her to the culmination of being a co-author of this book, as well as writing her upcoming books, "The Mean Nurse" as well as "The Newlywed Cookbook," a curated project of recipes gifted to her from family and friends around the World to feed her newlywed husband. Funny enough, her chapter in this book is on fasting and praying. Khaydeann believes that a fasted lifestyle is a powerful lifestyle.

Have you claimed the promise of you?
By L Tomay Douglas Varlack-Butler

What good would it do to get everything you want and lose you,
the real you? What could you ever trade your soul for?
Mark 8:36 MSG

This scripture is important to me because it connects how I have been able to claim the promises of God and my commitment to claim the promises of God continuously. As long as I have breath in my body, I will lean in and trust God. His word says, "many are the afflictions of the righteous, but the Lord will deliver them from them all." Yes, I commit to claiming the promises of God. Mark 8:36 is my starting point that asks, what good would it do to get everything you want and lose you, the real you? What could you ever trade your soul for? I believe in life that we need to develop a reflective practice, and for me, it allows me to sit in a space listening to what comes up in my spirit, in my soul, in my mind, and ask questions. In my academic, professional, and entrepreneurial experience, I found that I was surrounded by people who wanted to coach me, counsel me, and collaborate with me. However, what they had in mind was their bottom line. So, let's explore how Mark 8:36 connects. As a woman of faith, I discovered that true wealth exists in my relationship with God, Jesus, and the Holy Spirit. Therefore, I will share with you the promises of centering on your relationship with God and self. I'm not proposing this to be a self-help chapter or asking you to be selfish. This is a call to reflect on who you are according to your God-given gifts and purpose for His glory, the world to be impacted, and you to experience the benefits of being in alignment with God. As you read this, I invite you to ask yourself, have you claimed you?

Before we begin, let me introduce myself. I am a Black Indigenous woman, and my name is Latasha Tomay Douglas Varlack-Butler. I am the daughter of Dorothy Douglas and Melvin Douglas Sr. I am the granddaughter of Maggie Ree Harris Patterson of the Cherokee Peoples, Howard Patterson of the Blackfeet Peoples, and Melvin Pearl Douglas and Beatrice Glenn. I am a mother of two college graduates, Melvin and Kitana. I am the grandmother of Izumi with a grandson on the way. I am the wife of Darryl Varlack-Butler.

Most importantly, I am the daughter of God, a joint heir with Jesus Christ, and a student of the Holy Spirit. I am a survivor and overcomer. I am a substance abuse counselor, a social worker, an educator, a Restorative Justice practitioner, a consultant, and a coach. Most importantly, I am a truth-teller, even if that means telling the truth to me. The reason I open this way is the point of this chapter. You must embrace all of who you are and your multiple identities. For far too long, I kept trying to put myself in this neat box because I kept following a method of what worked for someone else because that was what I was told to do. However, it came from a mindset to mimic and add on top.

It wasn't a growth mindset; it felt more like a corner-cutting mindset. Of course, we can take a template and adjust. However, you are not a template. You are God's authentic living epistle. You are a book to read, and what good will it do to become someone else's book, try to duplicate their image, lose your soul for you to succeed? You are not a knockoff. You are the real deal. These are the things I grappled with and had to face in order to claim the promises of God. Can you have success without facing yourself? Sure, it's pretty much what the last president of the United States of America did. He succeeded in achieving his desired outcomes and goals; however, he was delusional about who he was, what he could do, and the impact of those he was supposed to serve.

Yes, your gifts can take you far because God gives gifts without repentance. However, I'm talking about claiming promises where your children's children will benefit from them now and later. I'm talking about claiming promises that will keep you in perfect peace because storms will come. The promises you hold onto to break the cycle of addiction, sexual abuse, and incarceration from your bloodline. I'm talking about the promises that not only bring healing to you but empower you to bring healing to others. Some promises will regulate your mind, body, and actions when you fully open your gifts. I'm referring to knowing who you are in God for those moments when people treat you like you are the exact opposite of a child of God. It's why my chapter is about claiming you, and the best way to do it is in relationship with God, our father, Jesus Christ, our savior, and Holy Spirit, our teacher. When you don't know who you are, when you don't spend time with yourself, or when you run from yourself, it moves you away from the promises of God. How can you say I know God when the way you practice principles in your business, community, and family do not align with those of God, instead it looks like those who have done it. I recall watching the series "I Quit' by Pastor Mike Jr when he said, we have bought into the lie of mimicking others around us. He said, you don't know what they went through and that they lost half their mind; I'd rather be me and uniquely different and go through or come out on the other side of success in wholeness. I thanked God because he confirmed this chapter through the preached word.

This was powerful because there was a time when I found myself wavering between what this person said I should do and what that person said I should be rather than ask God, seek God, spend time with God, and listen to him so he can reveal to me who I am. The interesting thing is my conversation with God went something like this. God, who am I? I'm tired of being like this and feeling like I'm supposed to show up in a certain way because that's what's expected of me. It didn't feel right. God's response: You are mine. The passage came back to me at that moment, reminding me that I have my being in Christ Jesus. I had to sit with that and think, okay, God.

I'm a joint heir. I have access to the throne. There's a ministry assigned to my hand, and while I may experience betrayal, heartbreak, and abuse along the way, it cannot negate that I am called for such a time like this. I responded to the call to choose a more excellent way, and the only way I can show love and love is by aligning with every part of me. I'm sharing this with you because it wasn't until I embraced all of me and my multiple identities that I was able to claim my voice and victory where I can now continuously claim the promises of God. Once you know who you are, you will walk in integrity, know the truth, and honor the power of your voice- to choose, forgive, live authentically, and love consistently. When you believe the promises of God and design your life according to who you are, you can claim the promises of God and receive the benefits of His blessing on the path He has for you.

As for me, I had to go back to God's word when He chose me and made the instructions clear. My heavenly dad chose me for something that I ran from for years. It's Isaiah 58, and the beginning starts with - cry aloud and spare not. Let's look at that passage. I'm going to use the message version because this is how God speaks to me. He makes it plain for me, and He makes it make sense.

"Shout! A full-throated shout!
Hold nothing back—a trumpet-blast shout!
Tell my people what's wrong with their lives,
face my family Jacob with their sins!
They're busy, busy, busy at worship,
and love studying all about me.
To all appearances they're a nation of right-living people—
law-abiding, God-honoring.
They ask me, 'What's the right thing to do?'
and love having me on their side.
But they also complain, 'Why do we fast and you don't look our
way?
Why do we humble ourselves and you don't even notice?'
"Well, here's why:

"The bottom line on your 'fast days' is profit.
You drive your employees much too hard.
You fast, but at the same time you bicker and fight.
You fast, but you swing a mean fist.
The kind of fasting you do
won't get your prayers off the ground.
Do you think this is the kind of fast day I'm after:
a day to show off humility?
To put on a pious long face
and parade around solemnly in black? Do you call that fasting,
a fast day that I, God, would like?
"This is the kind of fast day I'm after:
to break the chains of injustice,
get rid of exploitation in the workplace,
free the oppressed, cancel debts.
What I'm interested in seeing you do is:
sharing your food with the hungry,
inviting the homeless poor into your homes,
putting clothes on the shivering ill-clad, being available to your
own families.
Do this and the lights will turn on,
and your lives will turn around at once.
Your righteousness will pave your way.
The God of glory will secure your passage.
Then when you pray, God will answer.
You'll call out for help and I'll say, 'Here I am.' "If you get rid
of unfair practices,
quit blaming victims,
quit gossiping about other people's sins,
If you are generous with the hungry
and start giving yourselves to the down-and-out,
Your lives will begin to glow in the darkness, your shadowed
lives will be bathed in sunlight.
I will always show you where to go.
I'll give you a full life in the emptiest of places—firm muscles,
strong bones.
You'll be like a well-watered garden,
a gurgling spring that never runs dry.

You'll use the old rubble of past lives to build anew, rebuild the
foundations from out of your past.
You'll be known as those who can fix anything,
restore old ruins, rebuild, and renovate,
make the community livable again.
"If you watch your step on the Sabbath
and don't use my holy day for personal advantage,
If you treat the Sabbath as a day of joy,
God's holy day as a celebration,
If you honor it by refusing 'business as usual,'
making money, running here and there—
Then you'll be free to enjoy God!
Oh, I'll make you ride high and soar above it all.
I'll make you feast on the inheritance of your ancestor Jacob."

Yes! God says so! What a powerful passage! For years, I ran from what I was chosen to do: speak truth, live the truth, and represent the truth residing within me. However, it also meant becoming comfortable with being uncomfortable because it's difficult- at least it was for me when I didn't embrace myself. I thought I was honoring God's word. However, I wasn't a doer of His word because I was living the lie of mimicking the plan others had for me. After saying yes to why God chose me, I embraced all parts of me, the good, seemingly bad, indifferent, and inspiring parts of me because, in God's hands, He works it all together for my good. So, get to know you, allow being in the presence of God to remove the shame of your past mistakes or current reality. Now that I lean into Isaiah 58, I can show up as a Restorative Justice Equity Educator and Practitioner; I'm speaking out, talking back to the capitalistic values that have overshadowed the good work being done. Once I learned who I am, I understood not to fast with the bottom line in mind. I understood why some of my prayers weren't getting off the ground. I get why injustice must be addressed. I experienced the blessing of knowing lives are impacted for the good by the work I do. It's why the Lord placed in my heart how to help people be LIT, living inspired truth so communities can become livable again. To claim the promises of God, claim the promises of you and do it for His glory, not because someone you admire told you to. It's time we move away from the wonder of people with shiny cars, things, and a bag of tricks to keep you engaged with buying into the mimic lie. You are fearfully, wonderfully, and beautifully made, and there is greatness inside of you. The profits will come, the plan will come, and all the right people will show up; I just ask before they do, have you claimed you? You are God's first gift to yourself, and your voice is the world's first instrument. Each voice has a unique sound meant for a unique person. Embrace you because it's showing God that you agree with Him that He knows what's best for your life. Material things are a by-product of living in Christ Jesus; the intrinsic things such as your worth, dignity, and honor are hidden inside you.

As you finish this chapter, create your own reflective practice, and discuss it with God. The Lord is waiting to hear from you because everything you need, you have it. Therefore, set no man up as an expert over your life. People can coach you, but they cannot be Christ for you, and once you learn you, they will too. Know that God will show you who to connect with that is intentionally prepared by God to walk alongside you with wise counsel. I cannot begin to tell you how God is showing up and off in my life. Is it easy? No. Is it worth it? Yes, because I am worthy, and so are you. Here are some questions you can reflect on as you move forward in victory.

God is this (whatever you want to do/are told to do) from you? Is this in alignment with your will? Is this representative of who I am? Am I called to this work, or am I simply doing the work to make a profit? I have to tell you, the minute I stopped trying to mimic others and said yes to the hard ask of God, everything changed. I sat with myself, reclaimed who I am, and it's one of the major reasons I will leave no more unclaimed promises.

L Tomay Douglas Varlack-Butler

L Tomay Douglas Varlack-Butler is a Restorative Justice Equity Educator, Social Worker, a Substance Abuse Counselor, Consultant and Coach. Her work centers on healing, equity, and justice through education. Tomay is a facilitator with Restorative Justice Education, (RJ Ed), and is a Restorative Roots Collaborative member facilitating Participatory Action Research.

Tomay is the co-founder of WORTHshop Inc, a nonprofit to *affirm worth, change lives* and the founder of Responding Restoratively, to assist *with Critical Conversations to Build Community, Deepen Relationships, Heal Conflict & Return to Love.* She is an International Speaker where she presented in Haiti, led roundtable discussions with NGOs addressing violence against women, and facilitated restorative circles with adolescents impacted by HIV in Romania. Tomay is a PhD student at the University of San Diego and a resident *Restorative Justice* practitioner, project leader of HEAL Humanity Now! - *an equity and racial justice initiative*, facilitator on the RJ Certificate training team and graduate assistant at the Center for Restorative Justice at USD.

She has been cited in the media and did a TEDx Talk titled Just Riot, *a Restorative pathway to heal.* Her commitment to HEAL Humanity Now!, social and transformative justice deepens her practice and restorative lifestyle. Tomay's guiding principles are love, liberation, truth, justice, healing and being the mom of two college graduates and being a grandmother.

What color is your story?
By Kim Jones

I press toward the mark for the prize of the high calling of God in Christ Jesus.
Philippians 3:14

Whenever there is a challenge facing you, you must learn how to press on. Paul uses the analogy of a race to show that we are constantly striving toward our goal. God wants us to keep striving, keep trying, and keep moving on, trying to reach our goal. He wants us to press toward the mark. Whatever your mark is, press.

Dear God, I want to thank you in advance for the promise that I am believing you for. I know you have so many promises for me. As women, I know we have a covering. As your daughter, I have to ask what color is my covering? What am I made of? What is my desire in life? Every woman has a covering. Every woman has a past. Every woman wears many hats. This simply means that you gave us many tasks to perform.

God, we were told as little girls we were made of sugar and spice and everything nice. Well, as little girls, that sounds so sweet, but as a woman, it sounds bittersweet. The sugar in us may be nice and sweet, but too much sugar is not good for us, and the spice may not taste quite the way we want it to. Oftentimes as women, we have to constantly search for who we are. Some have been abused, whether the abuse happened in our childhood, adulthood, or marriage. Some women are fighting just to get by day to day. They are in a fight for survival. God, we have to keep asking ourselves what are we surviving today? We are trying to find the driving force that allows us to survive each day. God, what is our driving force? Is it our marriage, our children, our past, our ministry, or simply our life?

Women today wear so many hats. We do everything for everyone and do nothing for ourselves. Why do we do the things we do? Why do we run a race with ourselves, and no one else is running with us? Why are we in such a hurry? Why is my husband calling me? Why is the phone ringing? Why are the kids screaming? Why is the boss on my back, and why is the doctor telling me to slow down? Why am I having chest pains but can't call 911 until dinner is done?

As the Proverbs 31 woman is virtuous in business, so are we. She was clothed in purple linen. Colors represent so many things to so many people. Each color tells a story, and there is a story in everyone. Some stories are never told, and stories that are always told. Stories that are hidden and stories that are known, stories that will go to the grave without being told.

God, I know as a child we had dreams of who we wanted to be when we grew up. We dreamed such big dreams. We played dress-up and pretended to be a doctor, nurse, model, or even a television star, and we did all of this in front of a mirror. We saw exactly what we wanted to see in the mirror, and we loved it. But when the dress-up was over, we didn't love the little girl in the mirror as much.

When I used to hear people say that girls were made of sugar and spice and everything nice, I loved it. So little girls are the best of both worlds, they are sugar and spice and everything nice. As we began our passage into who we are today as women, we created a journey. I speak about a journey because we did not grow and get where we are overnight. It took years to get here. It took laughter, smiles, tears, and hurt. During this journey, we had to learn some things, give up some things, give back some things, and grow in some things. Our mother didn't tell us everything; some things were picked up along the way. There are so many roads that we may have taken on our journey, and we may have gone through some things on our journey, but as I stand here today, I can see that we made it through our journey because of your promise. There is always a going in, going through, and coming out. It was a journey, a struggle. It was a time of fear when the people of Israel crossed over the Red Sea as Pharaoh and his men chased them, but they made it. It may have taken them longer than they expected, but they found out on the way that it wasn't easy. When the enemy came behind them to destroy them, God, you gave them enough time to make it through, and then you closed the Red Sea. Thank you for that lesson, Father. Amen!

What is on the other side of your Red Sea today? Think about it because something that you have lived with so long becomes a part of you. It is stuck in your subconscious. That is why we have to be careful what we say and how we say it. As women building businesses, we want the easy road, but in reality, we have struggles, no support from family and friends, and it can be a Red Sea experience.

In 2019 I was doing well in a health and wellness company. However, I was doing the right thing but at the wrong time. My mother was sick, and I was traveling back and forth from Pennsylvania to New York, taking care of her, working a full-time job, and trying to work my side business. I often said I can't do this anymore. I'm tired of trying to make this business work. No one is supporting me; no one is buying my product. All the negative things kept flooding my mind. I eventually left the business after my mother passed away on February 26, 2020. I decided to rest because rest is all you need. Restoration and transformation come when you are well-rested. Restoration is going back to the original state. We cannot function if our mind, body, and soul are tired. When we are tired, we have a decrease in energy and motivation. We are not able to make good, committed decisions that will move us to the next level in our life.

God showed me that death and life are in the power of the tongue, so I had to speak differently. Don't allow your tongue to be the

77

thing that separates you from your destiny. There is destiny in everyone, so push ahead and see how far you can get. Push forward and live your dream. Push forward and find your place in life, your place in society. Press toward the mark. Like the virtuous woman was clothed in purple linen, we all have a color that represents us. What color represents you? What color is your story?

You are your color for a reason. It represents your unique ability to be women of color. What color represents the woman that you are? Is it the color that allows you to be proud of yourself? My confidence shows in my color, my self-esteem shows in my color, but what is my color? You are a virtuous woman. If you don't know what color you represent, do you truly have confidence? The confidence you need to pursue that business, to grow that business. Are you who you really want to be? Show the world who you are.

Is your color white? White shows purity and righteousness. When we were born, there was a sense of purity. The newness of a newborn pressed against the breast of the mother, looking into the eyes of innocence. Not a spot or blemish, just purity of heart not knowing the trials of this life. Not knowing of the many hats that will be worn one day. Is your color white? Are you still as pure as the day you were born? What is keeping your color white?

As we begin our journey into becoming a businesswoman, God, we don't know all the things we will have to face. I know that as we embark on the journey of business, there is a lack of belief. We must find the color that represents our brand. This color will determine success. But God, I know there are other things that we need your help with.

God help us with our lack of belief. Do we really believe that we can have the dream? O ye of little faith. Do we believe we can have the wealth? Do we believe that we are worthy? The reality of it is that we are our own worst enemy. When you don't believe in yourself, when you believe that nothing will ever work out for you, when you don't hold yourself in high esteem, you are working against your own life. There are so many things in life that will stop us from living the life we truly want to live. Things that will stop us from starting that business. Believing in ourselves can sometimes be the hardest thing we can do. Some things may have been told to us when we were younger, which stopped us from believing in ourselves. Words that have been imprinted on our hearts are still there today. Words that we have allowed to stop us in our tracks and won't allow us to move on.

God, I know the lack of belief in ourselves becomes negative thinking. It is our thoughts that will bring about action or NOT. It is our thoughts that will cause us to miss our season. Negative thoughts constantly creep in so fast that at some point, we begin to believe them. We must learn how to train our thoughts. God, I know there is no magic in you, and there is no magic potion that we need to train our thoughts. It's really simple, if negative thoughts come up, think positive. Don't allow negative thoughts to rule over you. We can control the things in our life by simply taking control. Pay attention to our thoughts and start to separate the good from the bad. God, you gave us the ability to decide what thought is important to our well-being. Add a "but" to our negative thoughts. For example, if we feel we are too far into debt and can't get out, we may say something like, I am so in debt I will never get out, but if I begin to save my money, I can start to pay off one bill at a time until I am debt-free. A small word like 'but" is powerful. It can change our negative into a positive.

God, you made us virtuous women. We can do all things through you that strengthens us. We will find the color of our brand. We will find that special gift that you have given to us. We will look deep within and stir up the gift within. If we want to be free of the things that keep us from our brand's color, we must stand firm and take control of our surroundings. God, you put us in the driver's seat of our life. We go where we steer if we are steering in the direction of nowhere, that is exactly where we will end up - NOWHERE! We must start moving in the direction of our prosperity. Start moving in the direction that allows our purpose to flourish. Start moving in the direction of our destiny. God, you are telling us that life is short, and we get caught up trying to make life happen and forget to live in the moment. Time passes by and we don't get it back. Live your life; enjoy your life, smile, laugh, and cry.

I encourage you, as women, to try to find your place in business and life to fight back against the things that hold you back. You only have one life; live it to the fullest. Live the life that you want, and not what someone else wants for you. God, you want us to live a life of happiness and prosperity. GOD, you said, beloved, I wish above all things that you would prosper and be in good health even as your soul prospers. He created this life for His people to praise Him and enjoy the fruits of their labor. This is your day, the first day of the rest of your life. This is the day that the Lord has made; let us rejoice and be glad in it.

Kim Jones

Kim Jones is a motivational speaker, certified personal life coach, bestselling author & playwright. She has an extensive background in the area of corporate training, empowerment coaching & career development. Using her gifts and skills and working in the capacity of a speaker/trainer has evolved her into a skilled facilitator with the ability to connect with & inspire any audience. Kim enriches audiences with her earthy, savvy, and charismatic appeal. Kim is also the Co-Founder of the LIFT Women's Conference.

Kim uses her talents and gifts to creatively write & express life through plays. Her love for writing is now coming to life through stage plays like Sis. Ruby's House and The Devil Made Me Do It. One day Kim will be on the big screen and producing motion pictures. Her commitment to God has allowed her to step out on faith and bring to life her vision of writing and producing.

No Good Thing Will He Withhold
By Glenda Kelly

But he said to me, "My grace is sufficient for you, for my power is made perfect in weakness." Therefore, I will boast all the more gladly about my weaknesses, so that Christ's power may rest on me. That is why, for Christ's sake, I delight in weaknesses, in insults, in hardships, in persecutions, in difficulties. For when I am weak, then I am strong.
2 Corinthians 12:9-10.

As I am awakened early this morning with the sun glaring through the blinds, I instinctively start to converse with God to thank him for a brand-new day, for His hand of grace and mercy, and for keeping me through the night. I thank Him that He has given me a new day and a new opportunity that I have the chance to get right. My day will not flow without first acknowledging the maker and the holder of the new day. My mind shifts instantly as my eyes fall on a picture sitting on my nightstand with the scripture, "For the Lord God is a sun and shield: the Lord will give grace and glory: no good thing will he withhold from them that walk uprightly. O Lord of hosts, blessed is the man that trusteth in thee."

This is one of the many passages of scriptures that, over the years, I have had to stand firm on, hold tight to, and not let go. As I read the passage, a memory popped into my thoughts. My mind drifted to when I was in grade school, and throughout high school, I was very shy and timid. I was not a social butterfly. I did not have many friends. Although I knew pretty much everyone, and they knew me, I was the wallflower. I was the standoffish one, but I was always very friendly and would go out of my way to help anyone I could, just for the sake of being included. Peer pressure will have you wanting to be accepted. I was never the one invited to the party, invited to go out and just kick it, invited to go to the movies, or even the girl to chat with on the phone. I was often the butt of cruel jokes. I was taunted and teased because of my big eyes, my big nose, my shyness, or just whatever. Kids can be cruel, but outside of school, I grew up in a very loving home where I was encouraged daily to be the best, do the best and treat people right. I was loved immensely by my mother, grandmother, siblings, cousins, aunts, and uncles. I was the baby of the family, and you know the BABY can't do any wrong. My values are strongly shaped by what I learned in my family and how I respond to others.

Although my family loved me, and they would go the EXTRA miles for me, I always had this sense of wanting to be accepted by my peers so much that it put me in a state of allowing myself to be in toxic and volatile situations that were not good for me. Those situations and the unhealthy need for acceptance caused me to be even more shy and timid. It hindered and stopped me from moving forward with things I knew I could do well. For example, when I was in middle school, we had a choir. I went to try out for the choir, and one of my classmates started laughing, saying, "Glenda, why are you trying out for choir? You know you can't sing." Her comments and laughter ushered in other classmates laughing and saying, "Yea!! You can't sing," so what did I do? I left and did not try out. Back then, I could hold a tune and even sang in my church choir, but her comments and the students laughing caused me to shy away and not do what I knew I could do and actually loved.

Fast forward, I graduated high school, went away to college, graduated college, and now was an ADULT with a child. My mother's friend asked me to do a speech for a program that an organization was having in a large prominent church. I prepared for the speech with the assurance that I could do it well because I knew I could say a speech well. I cut my teeth in a Missionary Baptist Church, and giving a speech was quite the norm for me even though I was still very shy and timid. My grandmother and mother ensured that I was on every Easter program, Christmas program, Usher program, Church Anniversary, Pastor's

Anniversary, Revival, or whatever program. Rest assured, I was going to be on it to speak and have it committed to memory.

I digress back to the story of being asked to speak at this event. I came into the church, and it was packed to the max. The pulpit was filled with clergy, the amen corners were full to the max, and every pew was packed. As I sat down, butterflies were already dancing in the pit of my belly from seeing the large congregation. I sat down and was given the written program. As I read over my notes and prepared for my name to be called, I heard someone behind me say my name with a little bit of surprise but more shock and disgust. The person said, "Glenda Kelly, Ha! Why do they have her on here to speak? She can't even talk." Then I heard another person snicker and say, "girl, I know that's right." As they had their conversation among themselves, I was sitting directly in front of them and heard all of it. I was not sure if they knew I was in front of them or if they did know, but it didn't matter. What matters is that their words caused an OVERWHELMING fear of not being accepted and not being able to do the job of what I had been called to do---- give the occasion speech. I sat there with tears starting to well in my eyes, my throat became dry, my heart was beating fast, I felt dizzy, and I felt with certainty that I would pass out. I became so nervous that I left my prepared speech on the pew when my name was called.

I was too embarrassed to go back to get it. So much was going through my head. I wanted to turn and run out of the church, but a divine intervention came when I thought I would run away from what I knew I could do. I heard in my spirit, "you have studied, you have prepared, and you can do this. Don't buck. Don't run. Just open your mouth". As I reached the podium, with my knees shaking and hand trembling, I had totally forgotten what I was to say. I stood for what seemed like hours, but I am sure it was only a few seconds. I mustered up enough bulldog tenacity to go back to my Baptist roots and upbringing of speech making and presentations. I could only remember what my grandmother and mother taught me to say, "To the Pastor, pulpit guests, officers and members of this esteemed church, visitors, and friends; it is indeed an honor to stand before you to bring you the occasion." After that, I don't remember exactly what I said, or how long I spoke, but I do know I spoke so well that the entire congregation gave a thunderous standing ovation. From the pulpit to the back row, literally, everyone was standing. My grade school principal was there as the Master of Ceremony. He said to me as I took my seat, "Now that's how you give an occasion speech, you just made me so proud to know you." The pastor of the church said, "Well, we can just say the benediction and go home now. Young lady, you keep on speaking, you keep on talking. You got IT." And then led the church in a second, more intensified thunderous joyous standing ovation. I walked away from that, knowing that I might be shy and timid, but I can do all things through Christ Jesus, who gives me strength. I may not be in the clique or the circle, I may not be accepted or celebrated by many of my peers, but I am loved by my Father, who cares so much for me that when I open my mouth, He will speak for me. I have often reflected back to that occasion speech, and it is engraved in my memory as a reference point of what God can do through you to bring him Glory

Father, I needed that memory of so many years ago as I prepare to move forward with the visions You entrusted me to carry out for your Glory. Visions that I know I am well prepared to carry out. Thank you for reminding me that You are with me and will never leave me to stand alone. Thank you for reminding me of your promises, and I don't have to allow the voices of others to hinder or stop me. Thank you for showing me how much you love me. You show me daily that I can trust You because You have proved to me time after time that You do not deviate from the promises of Your Word. You assure me in Psalm 84:12, "O Lord of hosts, blessed is the man that trusteth in thee. Blessed is the man who trusts in the Lord!" Thank you that with this promise, I can hang all the other promises of Your Word on. I am in awe of what You have done for me and are doing for me; the more I trust You. I am amazed that in trusting You, Your blessings are poured out on me. I rest in that promise and do not need to be anxious that Your blessings will not manifest greatly in my life. Forgive me for the times when I do not recognize Your blessings because I expect them to show up as I want them.

Father, thank you for showing Your love towards me and that Your Son Jesus finished work at the cross ensures me that I have a blood-bought right to every promise. I have only to pattern my life after that of Jesus Christ and walk the way that pleases Your heart. No good thing have you withheld from me. You favor me daily with your excellent goodness. Help me always to keep my ear to Your breastplate, to hear Your directives, and to move swiftly towards Your goodness. Thank you for being consistent in pouring Your blessings on me even when I am inconsistent. Father, help me always to have a heart of pure gratitude for all that You are doing in my life. Forgive me when I don't recognize that I have nothing to complain about, and I should always have a pure heart of gratitude for the very seconds You have given unto me. Help me always to radiate Your light to others. Help me to show a greater measure of grace to others even when I feel they have done me wrong. Help me to live out of the abundance of Your grace and mercy towards me. Thank you, Father, for the gentle reminders that even in my weakness, You are strong. I have the assurance of Your promise no matter the situations or circumstances; I am strong through you. Your strength gives me the courage to move bravely, unreserved, unafraid, and unbothered by the voices of my past, the voices of my present or future voices that want to speak uncertainty, doubt, fear, and unbelief. EVERY ONE of your promises is yes and amen.

To the person reading this, I hope this has given you some strength and courage to know that you can do anything God has assigned you to do. Stay close to His breastplate and listen intently for His voice. Embrace the fragrances of His promises and allow the aroma to saturate and penetrate every area of your life. Find a promise or two, or for that matter, get them all and stand firm on them, then watch how they will manifest in your life. The great effectual door is wide open, waiting for you to walk through it. Don't pay any attention to the adversaries who speak of the negative things that cannot be done. Remember, you have an exclusive right to the blood-bought promises of God's Word.

Always remember, His grace is sufficient for you, and His power is made perfect in your weakness. When the days come that the voices seem to over-talk you, remember to hold to the promises, hold on for the lives that are tied and connected to you. The promises are not just for you but for your legacy and the generations to come after you. You have a great inheritance to leave to the next generations, the promises of His Word. Everyone wins when you win when you embrace the promises like never before. You can do it. I encourage you today to just DO IT, whatever IT is that the voices of others are saying you can't do it. Whatever it is that your need for acceptance is saying you can't do, remember you have studied, you have prepared, and the world is waiting. I am CHEERING YOU ON!! YOU CAN DO IT; DON'T ALLOW FEAR TO STOP YOU FROM STAKING CLAIM ON EVERY PROMISE OF HIS WORD.

Glenda Kelly

Glenda Kelly is a highly skilled computer savvy professional whose passion is to provide quality administrative support and services to small businesses, churches, and startup grassroots organizations. She has over 35 years of managerial, education, and administrative experience.

In 2017 after over 20 plus years in public education, she transitioned from the classroom to operating her businesses, Be Sincerely Yours and Be Excellent Business & Tax Solutions on a full-time basis.

Along with this book project, she is a published author in three other anthologies, and she will release a book in early 2022 entitled "Kill it before it Kills You: Destroying the Enemies of Destiny."

She is the proud mother of one daughter, the grandmother of one grandson, godmother, mentor, and friend to countless youth that affectionately calls her "Mama Kelly." She loves the great outdoors, arts & crafts, and all things purple. You can connect with her at glenda@besincerelyyours.com

My Security Plan
By Jean-Marie E. McKay Williams

*"Do not be afraid; stand firm, and you will see the deliverance
that the Lord will bring you today."*
Exodus 14:13

This promise in Exodus 14:13 – that God will fight for His
children – is still valid today. When we find ourselves believing
this, we must remember that Moses said to the people as fear
shrouded their lives, and they macerated in unhappiness: you must
not be afraid; all you must do is stand still and watch God move.
There are times when we must be quiet but at the same time be
self-assured, optimistic, hopeful, and favorable to the successes
(be it monetary, a prayer answered, or a way made of no way) that
can be claimed through His promises. As I am saying this, I am
internalizing this promise which affords me the pleasure of fully
trusting God with the assurance that He will always see me
through and that some good will come out of this unfortunate
situation. He says He will never "put out a flickering candle" if
we stand in the hope of His promise. When God decides to do
something, He cannot be gridlocked by anything He has made or
created.

One frigid March morning, my place of employment announced
that it would be temporarily closing its doors and that we should
be prepared to work from home. Upon hearing this, hundreds of
thoughts began to flood my mind. The first thing is, "I am
doomed." Next, how will I be able to service the children
successfully? Knowing my predicament, I wondered what
implications remote learning would have on the students at the
end of the year? What would that mean for the state of education?
Thoughts of being incompetent, not knowing how to navigate or
disseminate information adequately, ideas of not acknowledging

my potential, and views of not knowing how to move forward caused me to pause for a moment and threw me into a state of becoming paralyzed with fear.

As I was internalizing all these alarms and sending myself into an emotional collapse, I did not realize that I was not claiming one of the promises to do ALL things through the strength of the Almighty. I was running on empty. I began my little secret prayer in my mind while trying to look brave as my colleagues strategized how to navigate this course. They had ideas, but I had none. They were astute in their knowledge of automation. I was mediocre. They were calm, but there was unrest in my mind. It was then I remembered reading that being "guarded in Christ that my secret prayers will be answered and that my faith will never be extinguished but will always bear enduring fruits." With this nugget before me, I began to believe that I should bring into play all the strength within me to achieve my success. I also thought that God would help those who help themselves until we cannot do otherwise but call on Him. The important thing that I learned from this experience was that God is not concealed from my human limitations. I was more capable of managing the situation than my thoughts of retarding my capabilities and victories.

Teaching remotely was arduous work. You come across every possible troubling issue: students not turning on cameras, logging off as they see fit, not showing up for class, and laying in bed as though it was a leisurely rest from labor. These behaviors were very troubling to the point where one could succumb to the pressures of life. But just as we ask God to direct our paths in all aspects of our lives, I found myself having conversations with Him quite often during that time of crisis concerning my fears and needs. "Do not be afraid and stand firm," He would say to me. "I am already working on a solution. Be diligent and finish what you have started." This promise can apply to you, too. God will always be at your side, for He is faithful. Having this promise in my pocket allowed me to understand that God never wants me to worry or despair because He is quite capable of being God all by Himself.

I used to think that I could have overseen remote situations and the blatant disregard for learning on my own, but now I know that the promise of not doing anything in my strength but having total reliance on God was vital. I realized then that those dark spots formed a plan for me. He brought about deliverance in the form of summer vacation – a time I could reenergize myself and become ready for another full year of the task ahead. He repeatedly said in His word that you will be an overcomer if you endure to the end, and He allowed me to overcome. Stand firm and watch Him deliver you. The year ended, and every accomplishment was hinged on the words that made my success possible. By holding fast to His promise, the greater His presence was in my life.

Standing fast while relying on the Lord's promises before us is very much decided and sure. You may ask why. It allows us to position ourselves for what is to come. He arranged the three summer months ahead and prepared me during that time to enhance and put in motion my newfound talent. The summer also allowed me to be expectant, and most of all, to anticipate a blessing that would follow in the coming school year. I was ready for service, and on that bright September morning, as I entered the hallway, I thanked God for the privilege to serve and to expand His kingdom. I was able to handle everything with His strength.

One reason standing on His promises is sure is because it permits us to be erect. For example, standing does not mean that you are motionless. What it means is that you are positioning yourself in an organized, marked position, setting, or adjusting yourself for the task ahead, then moving to make your way for your successes. Standing shows that you are confident, in charge, and is preparing for a change. To stand means that you are championing the cause of God when He tells us to wait and be of good courage. Lastly, standing fast and relying on God's word of honor means that you are sustained by the hope you have in Him and that He will come to your defense.

Another reason for standing fast and relying on the vows set before us and understanding that they are sure is that they allow us to wait on Him. Waiting requires patience, and I know firsthand what it feels like to wait. During the times of my crisis, many of my conversations with God dealt with being patient. Standing and waiting is not easy. However, it takes a particular kind of person with a specific kind of stamina to endure. I had to ask God to be patient with me while I had to be patient with the students. The Lord repeated the word "WAIT" twice in a single verse in Psalm 27:14. His repeating this word means that something important needs to be heard or something important will be spoken. If God is repeatedly telling us to wait during this period, we should be praying. What security! What a plan!

What surprised me most about waiting is that my prayers and the encouragement of my colleagues were strengthening me. Knowing that I wanted, needed, and expected a blessing kept me on this course to my breakthrough. "What blessing?" You may ask. By learning and experiencing God's power firsthand, one can stand and say that when God wants to bless you, He opens every entrance for you to receive His immeasurable offerings. When He says to you to stand, move, obey, and adhere to His voice, He will do far more than you expect. You must boldly claim all His blessings for all the provocations in your life and receive the full effect of His power. More than one year later, I am faithfully collecting the interest of seeing the deliverance that the Lord has brought me.

Although waiting and standing on God requires a craving, a feel for necessity, a desire, and longing for, it also means deliverance from your inactive state to getting up and making a move. It also means that through no power of your own you can claim assurance in Him that He will set you on the right path. That path, as you will know, will be productive. I guarded myself against apprehensiveness, cynicism, and pride and forged ahead in the power of His might. I eventually conquered all the odds and became successful over my fears.

Today, I can exalt the name of the Lord for being efficient, qualified, and skilled in all my challenges while exhibiting patience and understanding. My continuous expression of gratitude to Him is, "Lord, help me continue giving you the honor and praise for the achievements you have made available to me through your promises." When life's circumstance stands in my way, and as though God is not listening or His back is turned against me, I will not be discouraged. God will rescue me, as He has always done.

Many people think that claiming God's promises is complete in only one area of their lives, but I believe that it encompasses the gamut of where God wants to carry them. Faith in God's promises is something you can depend on. Dependence on God covers our entire being and circumstance, and that is reason enough for me to "rejoice always and to pray continually." (1 Thessalonians 5:16)

Seeing God's hand at work further solidified the over seven thousand promises He asked me to claim. Not seeing through the clouded vision of my dimmed insight of what it meant to stand firm and what was about to transpire at that time allowed me to grow. God created a path for me through all of this and assured me that I have no reason to fear but to stand firm, maintain my composure, hang on, and move forward. This promise remains my security plan.

People need to know that trying to be an overcomer in their strength defeats the purpose of having God change their circumstances. The primary reason for claiming all His promises has to do with you letting go and giving God a chance. Submission to God plays an integral part in the advancement of your cause and watching Him perform. I have come to know that I can rest assured and feel secure in God's movements and that He will always come through for me. I felt defeated, but God has made me a success. I felt ineffective, but God made me expedient. I felt anxiety and fear; God reassured me that all would be well. I felt impatient, but God allowed me to be indifferent to the things that

I could not have changed. So, my friends, "Do not be afraid. Stand firm, and you will see the deliverance that the Lord will bring you today."

Tell the Almighty your problems and consider how pronounced and powerful He is. When He intervenes in your crisis, be confident that you glorify Him for it and return faithfully to Him what is His. It will be at this time when the avenues of His insurmountable blessings will be opened up to you.

In conclusion, Hebrews 10:23 admonishes us to "Hold fast to the confession of our hope without wavering, for He who has promised is faithful." Because this is true, isn't it also true that what God says He will do that He will do. This promise is also the roadmap to my security plan in Christ Jesus - one that I will be standing on forever, and it is also one that He has given to me for keeps.

Jean-Marie E. McKay-Williams

Jean-Marie E. McKay-Williams hails from Old Road in Antigua, but she calls St. Thomas, Virgin Islands home. She holds a BS in Elementary Education and an MS in Special Education with a concentration in Emotional Handicapped Adolescence. She has been a New York City Public School Special Education teacher for thirty-one years and has garnered much acclaim for her bold stance on teaching and learning. Jean-Marie has been the Special Education Liaison and the Individual Education Plan (IEP) Teacher for the last four years at her school. She has also been nominated for School Board Chair at the Pocono Adventist Christian School and is a resolute Leader of the Women's Ministry Department at her church.

When she is not putting her all into her students and equally her church work, she's all building her business – **Celebrate It! By JJ** - creating her famous church masks, cake decorating and event planning along with her business partner Joyce Hippolyte. Jean-Marie spends much of her time reading, cooking, traveling, visiting Florida often to be with her parents, and volunteering her time at the Pocono Adventist Christian School (P.A.C.S). As an avid *Lifetime* fanatic, she feeds her addiction with her favorite genre, memoirs. Jean-Marie is a mother of two adult children, Jeynab-Sybil and Jeyden-Eugene. She and her husband, Everton, lives in Stroudsburg, Pennsylvania.

Keep in touch with Jean-Marie at celebratejj19@yahoo.com or jeyniedoe@aol.com

A Changed, Made-Up Mind
By Donna Renay Patrick

*"And I will give thee the treasures of darkness, and hidden
riches of secret places, that thou mayest know that I, the Lord,
which call thee by thy name, am the God of Israel."*
Isaiah 45:3

Mindset is everything. I remember when I was held back by my
own self-defeating, warped thinking. Can you relate? For too
many years, I unknowingly carried with me thoughts that worked
against my success in life rather than in favor of it. As an award-
winning author, transformational speaker/trainer, and radio host,
what I allow to capture my thoughts is important. Having a
healthy level of self-esteem has never been an issue for me, but
when it came to attempting great things that seemed outside my
comfort zone, that's when thoughts of "I'm not good enough,"
and fear began to magnify themselves in my subconscious mind.
With the help of my business coaches, I learned how powerful the
subconscious mind can be; but I also learned how to take victory
over it.

Even though a years-long career in corporate America brought a
decent living for me, I always knew God had more. Despite
having a semi-clear picture of what that would look like, I didn't
know that taking action would require a whole new way of
thinking for me. My comfort zone and I were joined at the hip,
and I would learn later how hard it would be to step out of it. The
question I had to ask myself was, "Do you love yourself enough
to do the hard stuff? If the life you want is found in your
uncomfortable place, will you do the work that is required to attain
it?" I have learned that (1) there is no growth in the comfort zone,
and there is no comfort in the growth zone; and (2) your personal,
God-given greatness will only surface from your uncomfortable

place. What follows is a synopsis of how my pain and my purpose collided to create a new perspective, renewed focus, and a redefined message to share with the world.

In Isaiah 45:3, God promises to give us hidden wealth in secret places and treasures of darkness. I had read that scripture many times, but God provided fresh revelation at just the right time through a sermon I heard from a nationally known Bishop in the Atlanta, Georgia area. At the time, I was too focused on what I had not accomplished, as opposed to what I had. I was in a dark place in my life and had no idea that this passage would bring a different perspective on what I was going through. Here is the truth: There is a *treasure* in you! I thought God was hiding things *from* me, but His plan was to hide them *for* me. God often uses the dark places in our lives to bring out the best in us and reveal potential that we never knew we had. God had to prepare me so I would handle the blessing well and exercise good stewardship over it. I was putting so much pressure on myself to perform rather than abide in Him and trust God's perfect timing.

When Job reminds us in chapter 33, verse 4 of his book, that the very breath of God runs through us, it caused me to adjust my thinking. I couldn't doubt myself anymore as I had in the past. God's breath, as well as His creativity, runs through me. This gave me a new determination to go forward with a changed mindset.

Second Peter 1:3 lets you know that God has already given you everything you need toward life and godliness. This means you already have what you need to do what He has commissioned you to do and live the blessed life He has created for you. There is no need to look outside of yourself to fulfill your God-given destiny. What I was looking for everywhere else was already inside of me. I can only conclude that I was afraid to tap into it.

Dear God:

I am so grateful to you for helping me understand that you really do give hidden wealth in secret places that I know not of. I thought the darkness around me was permanent when my business seemed to be going nowhere, and self-doubt began to creep in. You showed me that the darkness I felt was full of possibilities. I had allowed the darkness to cloud the truth that I was already wealthy in purpose and power. The treasures of darkness for me were not so much material but spiritual, mental, and emotional. My bank account was not looking good, and you showed me that you were so much bigger than my bank account. When I stopped reducing you to the size of my bank account, my peace returned to me. You reminded me that you are God over banks, mortgage companies, and any other currency, but I had to make my faith the main currency I approach heaven with – not dollars and cents. You reminded me that my bank account does not move you; my faith does. You are bigger!! Why would I believe otherwise?

I wondered to myself, "Do I really have what it takes to make millions doing what I love?" Rather than follow your directive in Second Peter 1:3, I looked everywhere else for what I thought I needed to make my vision reality. What I should have been doing was taking you at your word and using it as my springboard. Instead, I was looking outside of myself when you had already given me everything; I needed to do what you placed in my heart. Every day I was tripping over my own skills and gifts, looking outside of myself for the diamond mine when I *was* the diamond mine. I don't know why this was such an issue for me, but you were taking me to a new level, and I didn't see it. You were answering my prayer to teach me as I teach others. It required me to experience some darkness myself, so I could teach someone else how to navigate their darkness successfully and with a spiritually mature mindset. I knew what I thought it might look like, but the truth is, your ways are not my ways. Through this experience, you reminded me of prayers I had prayed long ago. God, though it seemed my faith had been on trial for what seemed like forever, you were maturing me for my next. There are stories of celebrities who get to a certain level of fame, and they wind up in drug or alcohol rehab, or worse because they could not handle the stress of the blessing. You don't want me to be one of those people. God, I am thankful that you are preparing me for my next.

During the past year and a half or so, in the midst of the COVID-19 pandemic, rather than lamenting a job loss and financial challenges, you gave me a mind to grow, learn, invest in myself and others, increase my giving, and continue pouring your Word into my heart. While other musician friends lost income because the churches, they served placed them on furlough without pay, my church kept me on staff, and my salary was not affected. God, that was nobody but you. Proverbs 18:16 was manifest concerning my work as a musician, which has always been bi-vocational. You said my gift would make room for me, and it did. The leadership at my church told me not to worry because my job was secure, and they made good on that. Lord, you took care of me even though my day job was now gone.

God, you have gifted me in multiple areas. You gave me the spiritual gift of teaching, the ability to speak to your people on various platforms such as radio and international podcasts, writing for Christian-themed publications to change lives, seasoned musicianship to lead and develop music ministry personnel, authoring award-winning books, and an anointing to lead congregations into your most holy presence in worship. Some of those things I never asked for were in your sovereignty, and you gave them to me. In my life, you continue to manifest two passages from the book of Proverbs – chapter 18, verse 16, and chapter 22, verse 29 - to reinforce your promise that my gifts will make room for me. I do not worry about being "in the right place at the right time" because when I stay prepared, you see to it that I stand before prominent people and not those who function in obscurity. Lord, by your Word, you have already seen to it that I am in front of the appointed people. God, I am thankful that my name has been spoken in rooms my feet had not yet entered.

Lord, Ephesians 3:20 became my go-to scripture because it freed me from small thinking. It freed me to believe you for the impossible when I was afraid to. Why was I afraid? It was because my faith was not at the level to trust God with my biggest dreams. I was in my head when I should have been standing on the promises of God's Word. As a friend of mine would say, "A promise is a promise." When I was limiting my thinking and my prayers only to what seemed possible in the natural, you caused me to raise my sights above "see" level. You strengthened my heart to believe you for BIG dreams and outcomes. I was already praying scripture, but you gave me fresh revelation on this familiar passage. God, that is one thing I love about you – you give fresh revelation on a scripture we've read many times before. New revelation brings a new level of spiritual maturity. I began to believe that you really will do exceedingly, abundantly, above ALL that I *ask* or *think*. But it also says, "according to the power that works in you," which is the power of the Holy Spirit working in my life.

Finally, God, I am grateful for a major game-changer to help me stand on your promises. Job 33:4 says that the very breath of God runs through me! Wow! How can I ever think I cannot accomplish all you have planned for me when I know that your very breath is in me? You created me in your image, which means you put a piece of yourself inside of me. That tells me that what you speak, I can speak as your representative and under your authority. That applied knowledge gives me the courage to pursue my vision and purpose unafraid.

Sincerely,
/s/ Donna R. Patrick
Donna Renay Patrick

To the woman reading this, I pray that you move into your destiny with a made-up, changed mindset on God's promises. May you not only believe God's promises for your life but act on them. Please be encouraged that changing your mindset is a process. I was so set on having a mindset shift that I began to pay more attention to what I allowed to contaminate my spirit; these old mental strongholds had embedded themselves in my spirit and were stealing my joy. It may not happen overnight, but you must be patient with yourself. Extend yourself some grace! Be determined to stand on God's promises even though circumstances may not be to your liking. Even though you are still doing the work and the results seem slow coming, celebrate even the small wins. For example, as soon as you *recognize* your thoughts moving away from God's promises for your future, that's a win! It's a win because you saw your mind going backward; you reeled it in quickly and began to seize the truth of God's Word. Wrap yourself in the truth of God's promises no matter what! Every positive mindset change is a win – celebrate that! It may seem like a small thing to you, but any time you change your mind from negative to positive and from fear to faith, that's worth celebrating. God wants to show you hidden wealth in secret places and treasures in the darkness. He wants you to experience His ability to do exceedingly, abundantly, above *all* you can ask or think.

> *"When nothing is certain, anything is possible."*
> Dr. George Fraser

Donna Renay Patrick

Donna Renay Patrick, M.A. is serious about walking in her unique purpose, and helping others walk in theirs. She is an award-winning author of two Devotional volumes - *At All Times*, and *It's In Your Praise*. She also co-authored three anthologies entitled, *The Perfect 7, Stories of Roaring Faith (Vol. 4)*, and *Be Refreshed*.

A passionate musician and choir director, powerful worship leader, and sought-after transformational speaker, she is a regular presenter at the Bay Area Church Workers Convention, serves on the faculty of The National Convention of Gospel Choirs and Choruses. and published a Commentary with The African American Lectionary. Donna also serves on the Executive Board of the Northeastern District Baptist Association, and is a certified instructor with the National Baptist Convention, USA, Inc.

Donna holds degrees from Bishop College, and Dallas Baptist University. She is based in Lewisville, Texas. Find her on Facebook, LinkedIn, and Instagram, as well as her website, www.donnarenaypatrick.com.

Black, Blessed, and Highly Favored – My Color is Not my Label
By T'Shawn Rivers

And the angel came in unto her, and said, Hail, thou art highly favoured, the Lord is with thee: blessed art thou among women.
Luke 1:28

A new commandment I give to you, that you love one another: just as I have loved you, you also are to love one another.
John 13:34

To be young, gifted, and black. That is who I was, raised on a tree-lined street in Brooklyn, New York; I always knew there was something special about my skin color. It was apparent in the neighborhood where I lived, in the church I attended with my family, and the hymnals that were sung by the gospel choir, like, "We shall overcome someday." Fast forward to the present, as a seasoned nonprofit and fundraising professional, I've had quite the journey striving to be the best that I can be. But the "skin I am in" did not make it easy for me to thrive along my career path with a silent investor and as an up-and-coming entrepreneur. From childhood to today, my journey to success has been tumultuous at times, but God has made a way for me to see my truth, fight for it, and survive through many ups and downs. This is a segment of my life's story of heartbeats and heartbreak, breakdowns and breakthroughs and how I survived it all with God's promise to bring me through. My blackness is not my label. I'm blessed with success because God's promise is real and has never failed.

I remember when I was little, my mom would take care of children. I didn't realize it at the time, but my mom was a foster parent to children who needed love and nurturing. On any given day, there would be three or four children of various ages and nationalities at my home, in addition to my older sister and two brothers. I would help my mom in any way that I could, even though I was just a child myself. I watched my mom give so much love to all of us, white, brown, it didn't matter. We were all brothers and sisters under one roof, and that was all I understood about skin color. Like crayons in a box, we all painted a picture of love and unity. Those were beautiful times. I thought life was the same in the world around me, but I was wrong. I learned at a young age that the world did not see me through rose-colored glasses as a kind, intelligent, vibrant person. Society labeled me, and I had to fight harder for what I needed from the world, and I had to trust God to bring me through.

From pre-kindergarten through sixth grade, I attended the Weeksville Public School, where the principal was married to the great, great-grandson of the late Booker T. Washington. The school was populated with mostly Black and Hispanic children. Each morning, after pledging allegiance to the flag, we would stand in front of our desks and sing along to the loudspeaker before class. First, we would sing the Star-Spangled Banner, and then we would sing the Black National Anthem, "Lift Every Voice and Sing." All the students who were mostly Black, like me, would sing with pride and energy. I have the fondest memories of my childhood, and even though I knew there was a difference between the color of my skin and others who were lighter skinned, it wasn't until middle school that I would have my first experience with racism, but that experience would not be my last.

On a sunny afternoon, a group of students traveled by city bus to Bensonhurst in Brooklyn for a track and field competition. At the time, my team, the "Thoroughbreds" were the top Black track team in the area. We were competing in the semi-finals in a 400-meter relay, and we were excited to get out of the neighborhood and have a chance to win the gold and advance to the finals. When we arrived and got off the bus, dressed in our tracksuits, ready to compete, every person in the neighborhood was white, and they looked at us as if we were from another planet. They did not understand why a bunch of Black kids were in their neighborhood. We just wanted to compete. Quietly, we made our way to the track field and started to stretch and prepare for the race. There were a lot of people looking on, cheering on their kids, and excited for the competition. Each team gave their all. There were four teams, including ours, and the competition was narrowed down to two. We were about to compete in the final slot for this competition; it was literally "white against Black." You could cut the tension in the air with a knife. As my team took the lead with me as the anchor for the final lap, it was obvious that the Thoroughbreds were taking home the gold. We were jubilant and proud of our success as we lined up to collect our medals. We were pulling ourselves together and collecting our belongings from the sidelines when someone warned us that there was a crowd of boys with bats and chains waiting for us to leave. We asked ourselves why we were being threatened, knowing that we won the track and field competition fairly. It was then that a member of a competing team said the n-word to us and told us we were not welcomed in Bensonhurst. In shock and fear, we exited the area from another direction and took off running towards the bus stop where we were dropped off. A few moments later, we noticed a group of boys running in our direction with bats and chains, yelling racial slurs and making threats. All we could do was run and not look back. We made it home safely, but our hearts and minds were scarred forever.

I learned a valuable lesson that day in Bensonhurst, Brooklyn. I realized that as I got older, my life was going to mean more to me than to the society I lived in, and because of "my skin," I would have to work that much harder to prove my worth and that I deserved to be in this world regardless of what I look like.

In the late 1980s, I landed a job at one of the most prestigious museums in the world. In my first interview, I had to take a typing and math test and answer a few questions on an application. Normally, an interviewee would take a test, fill out paperwork and then go home to wait to be called. However, my typing speed and math test scores were so high that I was asked to wait to meet the director of the fundraising department for the position I was applying for. After my meeting, I shook the director's hand, thanked him for his time, and I left, hoping for the best. When I arrived home from the interview, I had already received a phone call saying that I had got the job. That was the beginning of the best and possibly worse employment experience I would ever have.

After my first five months as an administrative associate, I was promoted to development coordinator, and my salary went up $5,000 annually – after five months! My aptitude for math and computers helped me excel within the department. I was the first and only person of color to achieve such success in the organization's history, and I was not taking my blessings for granted. Things were looking bright; it was a pleasure to go to work every day and make a difference. Then the management changed, and I was treated differently for reasons I could not understand, at least that's what I told myself. Working for someone who thought you were inferior because you were "different" from them was not easy. In my mind, I had earned the right to work for the organization. I didn't want to believe it, but it became apparent that my Black skin was the issue – not for me, but for others in the position of power who wanted to stay stuck in the past.

I remember going home after work, feeling dejected and wondering how I would manage at a place that didn't treat me with respect. I talked with my mom and dad and even prayed about it every night. My parents said Black people have always had to work that much harder for less to prove their worth. They told me I had a great job with benefits and to "hang in there" because God would make a way. But I knew there had to be more. My parents worked hard and retired from civil service jobs, but being from the south, they didn't understand that I didn't want to just get by. I was always an overachiever, competitive in academics, sports, and life. I wanted to be recognized for my talents, my intellect, and what I could contribute to the world. Just like any man or woman, regardless of color, I grew up learning about the racial justice movement and women's rights through gospel music, the Black history that was taught in my elementary school, and with role models like Shirley Chisholm; Mahalia Jackson; Shirley Caesar, and Fannie Lou Hamer, to name a few. This knowledge formed the person I am, and the person God made me to be. There had to be more than just fitting into someone else's agenda. I wanted to be appreciated and accepted for who I am, on the inside, not just the outside.

I continued to work at the museum, facing various challenges and bouts of underhanded racism, but being the tenacious individual God created, I persevered and managed to excel for twenty-seven years. In my 20th year, a milestone year, I was promoted to Director of Administration, overseeing a division of 65 staff in various roles within the organization. It was an extremely busy time, but now earning six figures and the respect of senior leadership and board members, I was in my element. My opinion and skills were constantly in demand, and I finally had a "seat at the table" regardless of my skin color. It was a long time coming, but I had arrived. My family was proud of my achievements. I was finally able to make a difference and leave a legacy for my children. I had worked for years at a higher level without an issue related to race or status. This was finally it! So, I thought.

In 2013 my direct supervisor, the Senior Vice President of my division, was retiring. It was bittersweet for my team because our division leader was amazing, and she had a heart of gold. She made it a point to leave a detailed letter for the incoming senior vice president about her team, our achievements, and what she envisioned for us going forward. The incoming senior vice president had a "reputation." It was a little unnerving for most of the staff, but we were hopeful. It became apparent in less than a year that all hope was futile.

After a year and a half, I had a new supervisor. I taught her how to do my job and hers, and a few months after that, I was forced to resign. My "services" were no longer needed. Just like that, after 27 years of dedication, sweat and tears, loyalty, and success, I was no longer needed. God, what did this all mean? Why am I being punished? Is this a punishment? I had so many questions but no answers and a broken spirit. I didn't understand that God had a plan for me to be better somewhere else. I couldn't see it at the time. I had to be completely stripped and broken to the core to see that God wanted better for me. For years, I had been loyal to the wrong people, and even though I always trusted God to provide what I needed, somehow, that job had become my god! I was so focused on proving that I was more than a "Black Label" to society that I was blocking God's blessings. He wanted me to take my talent and the lessons I learned and use them to create my own vision and business. This was His way of saying that there are people who need me to join with them and help them excel at their businesses. This was my "ah-ha" moment, but I had to be brought to my knees to see it.

In the summer of 2016, I had a new silent investor and a new tribe, the Lift, Launch Lead tribe of sisters and crusaders in the Pocono Mountains and from various states in the country. This opportunity to tell my truth of upsets, letdowns, and brokenness opened a door of opportunity that I did not know was possible. "I can see now, Lord, what you had in store for me." By partnering with the ladies of L.I.F.T., I now had the tools and support to excel with an entrepreneurial spirit! I never thought during my earlier years that I could be my own boss. It never occurred to me, but my parents used to "hustle" back in the day to bring in extra cash to support the family. My mom and dad could cook like nobody's business, selling dinners on weekends, and my mother would make clothing, bake cakes, and sell various meals during block association parties. My family always made a way out of no way, with various streams of income. I had the history, but I wasn't paying full attention to my purpose.

As women, especially women of color, we've been programmed to think less than when it comes to what we can be and what we must give. We suffer through so many trials and tribulations, and we stay stuck in pain because life can seem so helpless at times. I know life can be cruel. But we must remember, Jesus was persecuted, humiliated, tortured, and beaten for being a Jew who loved God's people. As great as our pain and suffering is and has been, there is no comparison to the crucifixion of our Lord on the cross.

This segment of my life story is to share my pain to purpose, my trials to triumph. I'm blessed to succeed because I have faith and do not give up. Don't let anyone dictate your happy ending. Your skin color is not your label. You are God's legacy. Keep the faith and never, ever give up. Thank you, Father God, for keeping your promises; I'm so very happy to share the blessings!

I praise you, for I am fearfully and wonderfully made. Wonderful
are your works; my soul knows it very well.
Psalm 139:14

T'Shawn Rivers

T'Shawn Rivers is a seasoned senior management, operations, and fundraising professional with over 25 years of experience. Currently, T'Shawn is the Director of Development and Campaigns, responsible for campaign logistics, Development fundraising and "friend-raising," as well as project management and proposal creation for foundations and corporations.

Prior to joining ABFE, T'Shawn was the Senior Director of Development and Partnerships at Race Forward and has an extensive history in the nonprofit sector which includes Women's Resources of Monroe County where she was a Director of Development and licensed Domestic Violence and Sexual Assault Crisis Counselor. T'Shawn also served as Director of Administration and Finance at the American Museum of Natural history, helping to raise millions of dollars over a twenty-plus year period.

T'Shawn majored in Business Administration at Medgar Evers CUNY, and is a published Amazon Best Selling author of two anthologies. She loves meeting people, learning new things and is an avid dog lover. T'Shawn is married with two adult children and a proud "Glam Ma" of three granddaughters and one grandson.

Bosom of God
By Chantel Rogers

"Have I not commanded you? Be strong and courageous. Do not be frightened, and do not be dismayed, for the Lord your God is with you wherever you go."
Joshua 1:9

There are times in every individual's life when they are frightened and distressed about the future.

I am standing on a promise from you, God, but I have a life of abundance, prosperity, peace, joy, and happiness. Lord, my God, there are many obstacles in my life that I have had to endure and would not win. Molestation didn't win because of your promise. Incest didn't win. Being stabbed multiple times and left for dead didn't win. Ridicule and being made to feel like nothing most of my life didn't win. Separation from my children while trying to protect them didn't win. Feeling depressed in despair, and even at one point, I didn't want to live anymore, but with your grace and mercy, I am standing on your word and knowing that you are my God. No matter what I have been through or what I will go through, you will always and forever be with me. I stand on your promise that you will love me no matter what. I stand on your word.

Lord, your word is forever true. Your promises that we can have anything our heart desires - love, marriage, children, an abundance of possibilities, the wonders of your world, and the wonders of your everlasting love. I've had to lean on your word and stand on the love of God to get me through so many obstacles in life. I've said this many times; we don't know why things happen to us. We don't know the outcome on the other side; we only know at that moment that it happened to us, and sometimes we even question why. But I stand on your word Lord.

I was worthless, a nothing. Your light has always shined in my life. Your light has always been the beacon that kept me going and allowed me to be who I am today despite what anybody thinks or decides. They want to decide on how I live my life or how I should have lived my life. I know that you and your word have always been true in my life. If my mother wasn't there, you were my mother, and when my father wasn't there, you are my father. When my husband was beating me, you were my husband. When my daddy wasn't there, you were my daddy.

It is in despair that you have always given me comfort. You wrap your arms around me and allow me to feel your warmth. I feel your love despite everything I've been through. You have given me the wisdom I need to become who you have created me to be. You have given me the direction and knowledge at 60 that was hidden in me at 16. You have given me everything I need. All the gifts and talents have allowed me to expound on the word to become the woman that you created me to be.

I stand on your word for every possibility that I could have as a wife with a husband who loves me, fulfilling my desire to travel all over the world and see your beautiful creation, allowing me to have a strong relationship with my children and my grandchildren, and leaving a legacy that they deserve. You say, "A good man leaves an inheritance to his children's children, and all the wealth of the center is stored up for the righteous." Guide me to make the right decisions and leave a legacy for my children and my children's children. Allow your love to flow through everything that I touch; allow your love to allow me to be who you created me to be and who you called me to be. You made me like no other, like the fingerprint or the thumbprint; there's no carbon copy of me because you created me.

I stand on your promises for health. I stand on your promises for healing - healing the little girl from everything that holds her back from being who you created her to be, even without the love of her mother. However, it was killing her not to have the love she always desired, to be the victim of incest, to give her body away; she was healing from depression and feeling like she was nothing. She didn't understand the things that happened in her life. She was healed from desiring the love that she felt she deserved. Today, I stand on your word. Lord, I stand on your word that no matter what I have been through and no matter what I will go through, you will always be there with me and for me. Thank you, Lord, for giving me everything you've given me because, without you, there would be no me.

I stand on your promise, Lord. I stand on your word that nothing will be void.

The Boogeyman, demon, sometimes keeps me up at night. Your word and your promise will always be my comfort and everything I need to succeed in this life. I thank you in advance for family, success, abundance, and the manifestation of your glory. You get the glory in my life, Lord. I give my life to you wholeheartedly. I stand on your promise that you can heal my family so that they too can feel your peace and know your love for themselves. Give them your peace and wrap your loving arms around them because if anyone can do it, you can. Give each of them hope in your love. I stand on your promise that if anyone can do it, you can.

I thank you in advance, Lord, for loving each and every one of us. Give us the guidance to stand in your word, walk in your word, seek your word and gain understanding and knowledge of you and your word.

I stand on your word that you don't put any more on us than we can bear and that the fruit I may have to bear has not been the best for some. Even in darkness, you were always my shining light. Even in the pits of my despair, your love reigned over me; you

117

kept me in your bosom. Even when I cried, you wiped my tears and gave me a safe place to feel love, comfort, and warmth. You sent strangers to love me when I didn't feel love. You set me apart from all the despair and gave me a new hope, a will to live, and your warm arms around me in a loving way like no one else could do. Aa a beckon of love that shines so bright in my heart, no one can love me like you, and no one has. You have been my saving grace my entire life. And I thank you, Lord, for loving me so much, for protecting me and sending your angels to protect me as your child.

Your promise of love, happiness, and abundance is granted to me because even if people say I don't deserve it or I shouldn't have it, your word says so much more. I thank you in advance for a man who loves me no matter what and will love me until death do us part.

Your word will be everything my heart desires; from this day forward, your love and aspirations for my life will manifest. Nothing anyone has spoken against me or about me will hold me back from being the best me that you created me to be. You allow me to shine on every stage I choose to share my gift and talents with. Every business venture I create while manifesting prosperity will leave a legacy for my children and my children's children according to your word, **"A good man leaves an inheritance to his children's children."**

Every gift and talent you have given me, every idea that you will allow me to create, will bless me and the people around me. The numerous business ideas that you have given me will live and not die. Everything you created me to be will be. Your light in my life will shine. Allow me to see your love on a whole other level. My riches and gold will not only be in heaven but also on Earth because you said so. My heart's desires are the desires you have for me. I thank you in advance for a loving family and loving husband that loves me all the days of my life. We will serve you together, travel the world talking about your blessings and be a blessing to others.

So, we say with confidence, "The Lord is my helper; I will not be afraid. What can mere mortals do to me?"
Hebrews 13:6

I have been afraid to shine, worried about other people and their judgment against me. One of the people I thought should have been my biggest support and cheerleader has been my biggest and longest setback. My life was based on what they said to me, and my inner mind has believed it even though I constantly tried to remove self-doubt and push through. I have always had these delicate setbacks that caused me to be stagnant. We are through with feeling like we haven't made it to our full potential. We are going to rise to the top and get everything that God has promised us. I declare and decree that my life will be what God says it can be and will be done. No matter what the chatter has held you back, take charge and know that God has given you everything you need and want. All you have to do is move out of your own way and allow the promises of God to manifest in your life. We all can do it. Remove yourself from the worry and let your light shine.

Repeat after me - I will have everything that was taken away. I deserve everything that God has for me. I am not allowing anyone to hold me back from the greatest life I can manifest with God's promises.

Release it all and give it to God. Rock yourself in his bosom to find comfort in him. Believe in yourself. Your promises are awaiting you. When you think about the goodness of God, His promises are beautiful and rewarding. He makes a way out of no way. When money magically connects to you, and all your worries are put aside, he has made a way out of no way. That's his promise, and no matter how it looks, it is always a rewarding and glorifying feeling to know that God matches what the word says and that every need will be met. Even when it looks like your back is against the wall and there is no way out, he finds a way to show how much he loves us over and over again.

Take some time to think about how good God has been to us. I know He has been good to me. When I didn't know where food would come from to feed my kids, there was a knock at the door. When the bills were due, and I didn't know how I would pay it, a client called, or someone felt the need to bless me. Reflect on the goodness of God and believe that every need will be met, and his promises will manifest. There is no other love like the love of God. We should rest our minds in his love and feel the presence of God and his promises for us.

Chantel Rogers

Chantel Rogers challenges her clients to live their lives with purpose, courage, and strength. Her focus is personal development, business coaching, marketing, branding, and training. Chantel captivates her audience allowing them to see the bigger picture to reach their full potential. She believes everyone has a gift or gifts that were given to them to be successful. Chantel teaches entrepreneurs to become leaders with a CEO mindset. You will get results that will elevate your business. Her coaching programs help you transform your life and take a leap into your passions and carefully help you to develop your gifts and talents and turn them into your reality. She successfully helps men and women build. To book for speaking engagements, visit www.chantelrogers.com. To dig deep into your gifts and experience a life change, visit www.releaseyourenaissance.com.

The Promise of Purpose
By Térésa Scotland

"being confident of this very thing, that He who has begun a good work in you will complete it until the day of Jesus Christ."
Philippians 1:6

You aren't here by chance. God intentionally created you in the way He did because He is deliberate about who He wants you to be and what He wants you to do on earth. This can be hard to grasp when so much of what we do is dictated by how we are positioned in the world. As wives, mothers, employees, church members, and friends, we often follow the to-do list someone else set for us, neglecting to see that there is anything remotely possible for us outside of these roles and how we can thrive apart from who we are to others. We may compare ourselves to those who seem to do everything with such effortless grace and ease while we struggle with our day-to-day tasks. But God has created us all differently, for different purposes and seasons. Imagine if the women in the Bible could have swapped roles. Esther most likely couldn't have done what Mary did because she didn't live Mary's Life. She wasn't chosen for that assignment. Don't get so caught up in comparing your struggle to someone else's success that you discount their learning curve or how God works in their situation to help them to thrive.

God set each of us up with a specific set of abilities, talents, and personality traits that He plans to use to achieve His purpose. If you think you're unqualified, or there's nothing special about you, know that God specializes in using the unlikely, the broken, and the lost for His glory. The things you dismiss about yourself could be exactly what He will use – even your mistakes and your pain. Hagar was "the other woman." The woman with the issue of blood was shunned during her suffering, and Rahab was a prostitute.

God used each of these women to illustrate the authority of His anointing, the power in His presence, the restoration in His forgiveness, and how His purpose always prevails.

We are all given the same advice growing up – go to school, learn all you can, and get a good job so you will have a good life and be happy. Life has taught many of us that it isn't guaranteed to work that way. Take a few minutes and review your life's resume. I encourage you to write it down. You might recognize many achievements, and now that you've written it all down, you might think you can do even more. It's tempting and natural to seek to fulfill that longing with more achievements. Looking deeper, we will see that what's missing isn't a what but a why.

I want you to think back to your childhood. What was the thing that gave you so much joy it caused you to lose track of time? I have loved to read, draw, write, and talk for as long as I can remember. I would sit for hours with my sketchbook, planning my fashion collections or recording interviews on my father's briefcase tape recorder. I don't know where he got that thing, but he wasn't a Secret Agent, I promise. I remember sitting in my bedroom, microphone in hand, hosting interviews on my imaginary talk show and talking about my upcoming plans. I had so many plans! And then, life happened. Most of us don't live a fairy tale life. As much as God has blessed us, some of us have a litany of mistakes, shortcomings, and ill-advised decisions that have led us to walk along strange paths. Some of us lost direction. Some of us were ambushed by life's circumstances, and through no fault of our own, found ourselves lost, wandering and frustrated, walking in circles. Some of us got injured, believed ourselves too weak to walk any further, and settled right where we stopped. This was me – settled, frustrated, and feeling stuck.

When I got married, I was working in a position that worked well for our lifestyle. I enjoyed my job, earned a decent salary, and had good relationships with my team members. There was room for growth, and things were looking great. My husband decided to move, and so I couldn't keep my job. It was bittersweet, but I was looking forward to what our new life would bring. I had the opportunity to stay at home with our then three-year-old daughter, and we soon had another child on the way. God blessed us that my husband's salary was enough to provide for our family, so I didn't need to work. By the time our new baby was about a year old, I had started to feel the itch to go back to work. I had been used to working, and it felt uneasy to be at home, doing nothing (as if caring for my family was nothing). I felt there was more I could do and earn. I didn't realize it then, but that discomfort was the beginning of the decade-long tug on my heart, pulling me to my purpose. Here I was, with two small children and a husband who provided for us. We were in a good place. Things looked good, but I still felt something was missing. It was a difficult time because when I looked at my blessed life, I thought, how dare I be so ungrateful when I am so blessed? I pushed those feelings down, and I tackled the to-do list, day after day, but that feeling sat in my spirit. If you've ever felt a similar tug, I've written a letter to God, praying for you.

Dear Lord,

Thank you for the woman reading this right now. Thank you for her life. Thank you for every blessing you have given her. Thank you for all the potential you knitted into her when you created her in her mother's womb. Thank you for allowing me to speak to her heart and to tell her how dearly loved she is by you. Thank you for her family, her health, her job, her home, and her purpose. Thank you for placing her in my path. Thank you for keeping her for such a time as this and opening her heart to be receptive to Your transforming power.

Thank you for her desire to know Your promises by reading this book. Thank you for the tug on her heart, letting her know that there is more to her life than what she has done or who she has been. Thank you for hearing her when she couldn't speak up for herself. Thank you for understanding when she looked strong on the outside but was falling apart on the inside. Thank you for keeping her mind. Thank you for all the desires you placed on her heart. Help her to see that it's okay to want more than what life is giving her. Help her to know that You called her, and You have already equipped her to carry out Your plan for her life. Help her to see that she isn't strange; she is set apart. Help her to know it is her uniqueness that makes her special and help her to own it as a rare gift from You.

Lord, show Your specific purpose for her life. Give her revelation, strategy, resources, and determination to see Your purpose for her life fulfilled. Uncover her unused gifts and unveil the dreams she covered up and set aside. Cause the spark in her creativity to be rekindled and cause her light to shine so brightly for You that Your Name would be lifted up. Cause her to thrive, using all You have placed within her. Cause her to be a beacon of hope, an example of godly womanhood, and a nurturer of her own promise and the promise of others.

Bless her in her family life and promote her in business. Bless the work of her hands and elevate her in status as she deepens her relationship with You. Help her to seek You out as her Chief Advisor in all business matters and lean on Your wisdom, Your directive, and Your timeline. Help her to be obedient to Your calling and Your commands and strengthen her arms for the tasks You have placed ahead of her. Thank you for her next steps of faith. Thank you for taking her to new levels and thank you for the grace to handle the promotions that will come her way. In Jesus' Name, Amen.

My dear friend, God has already designed everything He wants you to do for Him. One of my favorite scriptures is Ephesians 2:10, "For we are God's workmanship, created in Christ Jesus to do good works, which God prepared in advance for us to do." It is a scripture I found while looking at my own life and seeking to pinpoint the thing God prepared in advance for me to do. As I meditated on this scripture, it showed me that I was feeling unsettled because I chose to settle. I did the things. I went to college. I got a good job. I paid my bills. I even paid my tithes! I worked hard. I got bonuses and raises. So why wasn't I satisfied?

God wanted to bless me with more, but it wasn't in the way of achievement or finances but in who I needed to become.

I had become resentful of the blessings in my life. The joy of being able to serve my family wasn't there. Instead of feeling happy to take care of my home and my family and enjoying the tasks my day brought, I endured them. I started a personal Bible Study a few years ago, and it changed my perspective on God. As I journaled God's word and His revelations to me, my mindset shifted to one of gratitude. As my perspective changed, so did the possibilities that opened for me. Ministry opportunities became available. I was called on to do new things. I started selling my work, and most of all, I owned who I am in Christ. That made all the difference! No job, business, or achievement could replace the knowledge that God put His purpose in me for me to walk out. I had a new sense of responsibility. I owed it to God to use the talents He gave me. But how?

I want to share an acronym that describes the steps I take in my own life, and can help you as you walk the path to the purpose God has for you:

P is for "Practice"

Practice God's Presence – Invite Him into every aspect of your life so that He can guide you in everything. It's easy to want to compartmentalize life into the God areas and the areas we want to handle on our own. Ask Him continually for direction and guidance. As you spend more time with Him, you will get to know Him better, and you will get to know when the urging in your spirit is from Him or yourself. As I type this, it's 2:32 am. God woke me and gave me this message. I know His voice by now. I know when He's leading me and when I'm trying to convince myself of something. Trust me; if it was my voice in my head, I would have convinced myself to close my eyes and go back to sleep. But the call of God is one you can't shake off. The voice, no matter how quietly It speaks, has the power to move your entire being to obey.

U is for "Unlearn"

Study your Bible. Unlearn what doesn't serve God and thus doesn't serve your life's purpose. Learn what is true about God and what He has promised to you. Ask Him to show you His Truth, so you can discern which direction to take. Have your own personal Bible time and ask God to remove the beliefs that don't serve Him or your purpose.

R is for "Rest"

You've had enough stress in your life. Rest on God's Promises – His promises are yes and amen. We don't have to second-guess God... ever. He has promised to give you rest and ease your burdens. Take the necessary time to shut down. Your mind, spirit, and body need time to recuperate and be refreshed.

P is for "Patient Preparation"

God can give you a sudden blessing, and sometimes He takes His time. Wait and expect to be blessed in God's perfect timing. Make room for His blessings in your life by working with Him to eliminate what doesn't align with His will for you and build a life guided by His blueprint, the Bible. When His blessings come, they will fit if you have made room to receive them.

O is for "Open"

Open yourself to what God can do when you have fully submitted to Him. He can do exceedingly, abundantly above what you can ask or think, through the power of His Holy Spirit working through you. Think of your biggest, craziest dream, and then make it bigger. God can do way more than that! Don't be discouraged by how things look. Keep your eyes on God. Like the little child you used to be, have the childlike faith in God that assures you He has already equipped you to be and do everything He created you for.

S is for Submit

Submit to God. Give every area of your life to God for Him to use all you are, all you have, and all you have been through for His glory. Don't worry; you're going to look better than what you've been through. Let go of your own agenda and take on the work of God, even if, and especially if it means doing something new. The awesome thing about working for God is that He has already hard-wired you for your purpose.

E is for Evangelize

Not everyone is called to preach or teach, but every Christian is a representative of Christ. There is someone right now who is watching how you handle adversity and how God brings you out. There's someone else who has no idea how you do your life. How will they know God brought you out if you don't tell them? Walking in your purpose will serve those God sent you into the world to bless.

I'm living today with a sense of purpose I didn't have ten years ago, or a year ago, if I'm honest. God has done so much in my life. I couldn't fill this book with the blessings He has given me! I treasure my purpose and the peace that comes with it. There is such a peace that envelops me, even in moments when I undertake something new, and leads me with confidence into the next opportunity. God is so good!

When I launched my website, www.amalya.org, it was a way to sell my creations and share my faith through words of encouragement in my blog. I thought that was it, and for a while, I was sailing smoothly along, but God had more for me to do. As the first whispers of COVID-19 and quarantine life began, that familiar discomfort that signaled, "there's more" couldn't be ignored. I set out on a journey of intentional personal growth and was led to an online challenge hosted by an accomplished motivational speaker I've been following for years. Her challenge opened my eyes, and I saw the necessity of answering The Call on My Life. I had been skirting around it for too long, afraid to dive in and implement the ideas and strategy God had already qualified me to execute. The wonderful thing about truly seeking God is that you will find Him, and when you do, you will find yourself and your purpose.

I'm writing this chapter while on the cusp of launching my VISION Sequence. It's a 7-step sequence that empowers you to imagine, believe and act in faith to make your vision for your life a reality. My vision for my life is so much bigger than it was just a year ago. I now use this sequence daily, and I'm excited to share this with as many women as I can. If you're feeling stuck, insecure, and unqualified to work towards a dream that's bigger than you are today, and you want a clearer vision for your life, you can find more information on my website. I would love to guide you to see more of what God has in store for your life and see it become your reality.

In Jeremiah chapter 1 and verse 5, God told Jeremiah He knew him before forming him in the womb. Think about that. Jeremiah's purpose was in place before his life began in his mother's womb. Even though you are a woman, you aren't any different from Jeremiah. Don't discount God's plan for you, thinking there's nothing special about you, or that too much has happened, you've wasted too much time, or you're damaged goods. Living life and dealing with all it brings can cause you to be distracted from God's intended plan for your life. There will be pain. There will be disappointment, suffering, and tough times. And there will always be God. There will always be His grace, forgiveness, and power. His purpose didn't get deleted because life distracted you with a detour. Daughter of the Most High God, you can have it all. God promised you an abundant Life. Claim it!

Térésa Scotland

Térésa Scotland is a Jesus-loving wife, mother, artist, writer, and leopard print enthusiast. She is passionate about helping women appreciate their attributes, affirm their value, articulate their dreams, act authentically and access abundant life, by connecting them with God through art, design, words, and mindfulness.

In October 2021, she launched The V.I.S.I.O.N. Sequence, a guided method for creating faith-fueled goals based on God's word. The V.I.S.I.O.N. Sequence is available as an eBook on her website, www.teresascotland.com. You can find Térésa at the Instagram handle "@aafrotee", where she goes live with a daily encouraging word, and shares glimpses of her personal life.

Under her brand Amalya Creative, Térésa makes high-quality tote bags and decorative accent pillows, among other items, all with a scriptural theme, to remind her clients of God's presence. She is active in ministry, serving in an intercessory prayer group, and as a liturgical dancer, among other roles. She is driven to fully live out her vision with her husband and children and wants to encourage you to freely and confidently walk in your God-given purpose.

Crazy Faith
By Joanna Smith

I can do all things through Christ who strengthens me.
Philippians 4:13

Do not be weary in well doing for you shall reap if you faint not!
Galatians 6:8-9

God will never leave you or forsake you; if he brought you to it, he'll bring you through it, no matter how it looks, keep putting one foot in front of the other, and keep moving. All your strength will come from Him.

Crazy Moves – Quitting my 9-5 in the midst of a pandemic.

In the eighth grade, I vividly remember my dad picking me up from school. I was such a daddy's girl. I loved exercising, running, lifting weights, and doing mathematics. I was a different kind of girl, which was fine with my Poppa and me. My mom was an angel. She would glide into the nursing offices and hospitals and have all these delightful and sometimes crushing stories of how she would help to bring people back to life or back to their limitless selves. I enjoyed these stories, but I wanted to create a different story of my own. I wanted to make one of dominance and power, roads, bridges, skyscrapers, and foundations. "Foundations," "you ask? Yep!

This particular day I was on my way from school. My dad had come to collect me from the train station. He was always on time, so I liked when he picked me up (I'm laughing inside just in case my mom reads this). This particular day I was tired, and Dad was asking some questions about school. I answered groggily as I was slumped over on one side looking through the window. Wow! To my surprise, there was a green piece of metal sticking out of the asphalt. What was this? Promptly, I awoke from my groggy posture to see a sign that said, men, working on the road! I had an idea. I said to myself, "as soon as I get home, I will hop on the computer and research men working on the road." I remember hearing that dial-up on AOL. It was the fastest it had ever been! I typed in men working on the road, and civil engineering popped up! "That's exactly what I'm going to be," I said to myself. Next time there will be a sign that says, women working on the road. My goal was etched very clearly in my frontal lobe from that day forward.

Decisions, decisions, decisions. My goals actualized quickly. I had an internship in Cancun, Mexico, and Jamaica, West Indies, before 17. I entered Germany as the only girl from my university chosen for the U.S. Army Corps of Engineering European district internship in 2010. What an amazing journey as a civil engineer. I met the four-star general, General Kip Ward, for dinner at his home, as an engineer and guest pianist at such an establishment.

I completed my degrees in Civil Engineering with a concentration in Geotechnical Engineering from Morgan State University and Johns Hopkins University, my dream school. As a mentor and secretary for the various engineering programs like National Society of Black Engineers (N.S.B.E.), American Society of Civil Engineers (ASCE), Architecture Engineering Construction (A.E.C.), Deep Foundation Institute (DFI), Geo-Institute, and at one of the largest engineering firms in the country; I saw how powerful mentorship truly was. Mentorship allowed me to work on the Hunts Point project as the Geotechnical lead to begin the project as the Subsurface Investigator and Inspector as we broke ground to retrieve soil samples to create a design for the foundation for this $1.8 billion project. Trucks, cars, trains, and various loads that the surrounding structure would impact were considered. I worked through Super Storm Sandy as the homes and the subways flooded beyond quick repair. Our team designed foundations and Gibson walls for the M.T.A., private airports, and projects in Quebec and Trinidad. While engineering, my team and I published four engineering papers, we were able to speak at conferences, sit on committees to invite speakers to the annual conventions, and was I was elected as a new face of civil engineering in 2020, as well as one who sat with the executives of the company to etch out plans for diversity and inclusion. I was not only the woman working on the road, but I was creating an impact! The eighth grade Joanna who wanted to be a civil engineer was very pleased. Wow! Five years and all of that accomplished. That's enough, right!

What I didn't tell you was that the first two years working as a civil engineer were some of the roughest moments of my life. I felt like there was a demon with no clothes walking around personified as a superior in the space where I had so many opportunities. After two years of working as a civil engineer, I was ready to go! "No, No, No," my mom said, "just wait." At this point, I was doing all the interviews I could to get away from this situation. Through it all, I wore a smile, but boy was I brewing!

As a professional pianist, I knew that I wanted to bring out mathematical concepts through music. The vision was clear in 2018. You will blend both mathematics and music to reach thousands and millions of children worldwide and set a foundation for a different mindset geared towards Science, Technology, Engineering, and Mathematics (S.T.E.M.). Wow, how do we diversify the field of S.T.E.M. with leaders, program managers and create a pipeline effect from elementary school up to corporate or entrepreneurship? Let them know about the I am, that I have sent you! The company will be called Daleysmithininc. It is a blend of your mother's maiden name, the angel nurse, and your surname from your dad's side, the dominant side that you desire. When I received this message, I cried so hard for two weeks. I had a prayer partner that started a reading on the move of the Holy Spirit. I knew that the time would come for me to start my very own company. I was doing it through math and music, but it was just me. How God? How do we expand this? How????

The 2018 vision manifested in 2021–No Way! Yes, way! In 2021, I quit! I sent the email on Friday, January 8, 2021, at 9:30 A.M. The pandemic grabbed me in its arms and rocked my mind awake, demanding conclusions that were hiding in my frontal lobe. My now boyfriend, at the time acquaintance and music partner, helped me make this BIG decision I was planning three years ago. He called me at midnight on the way from his house and said, "Wherever you are, please stop." Mind you, it's midnight in Brooklyn, NY, and I'm at a gas station waiting. Boldly he pulled into the gas station, hopped out of his truck, and quickly sat down in the seat next to me with one foot hanging out the door. Timidly he looked at me. In my mind, I was wondering what he had to say? He started looking up at the roof of the car, playing with his fingers, and then proceeded to look over at me and say, "I like you." "Ok, that's good to know," I replied. He followed his statement with, "You don't have to do anything with that information. I just wanted to let you know before I leave for Andrews University in 7 hours." Can you say relieved! My next question was, "can I touch your hair"? So random, I know, right. The truth was that I had been looking at his luscious, beautiful locs every time we worked on music together for the Blue Room Music series; however, there never seemed like an appropriate time to ask such a question. I wasn't sure how my interest in the fabric and texture of his hair would add up as a question worth asking or a gesture to explore, but now I had my chance. I asked, and he said, "yes" Finally, I touched the tip of his loc, the one closest to me. His hair is definitely a mixture of a 4b and 3c hair texture. I continued our conversation by telling him that his bold move was the sign of courage I experienced and would be a catalyst for what I had been brewing over for the last three years.

I quit! I was working on a project in Ticonderoga, New York, for 333 miles of Power and energy lines to be drilled vertically and horizontally. I was asked to be on assignment out there for one month, about four hours north of my home. The January air was crisp and clean! It was time to begin walking in the vision of the Science, Technology, Engineering, and Mathematics company revealed to me in 2018.

Doors began opening by mid-January, and no later than January 18, I received a call from a program my sister used to work with asking for me to come and be the lead S.T.E.M. instructor for 60 children in grades K-5. It was amazing. Just like that, another door opened. I had five groups of students and a curriculum of solar power and circuits that I created based on a physics class in college. Some of these students had never been a part of a science fair before. The students were tasked with creating a model of a solar-powered city using the solar panels and battery kits to create a circuit using L.E.D. Christmas lights as the lights for the houses and businesses. They created a landscape and project plan of what they wanted in their city. They wanted an airport, stores, apartments, a statue of liberty downtown, and a playground. This was the ask of the kindergarten class, and they constructed a masterpiece in eight weeks. Two days a week, the students had a 45-minute S.T.E.M. session which included an activity period of completing the city and an informative session on new information. The first-grade class was tasked with creating excel spreadsheets for all the project materials used for the assignments. I was so excited about this! Other students were asked to code using Scratch to create a presentation and game to show how L.E.D. lights worked with regards to the circuit that they were building. The rich curriculum was high quality. The teachers were in awe of what was completed in such a short time. It was time to move into the next portion of the vision, facilitating my very own Summer S.T.E.M. Camp. This one would run as the next leg of the vision. As a runner, I can relate to the team of runners that come together to win a 400-meter race. In my eyes, we completed the first 100-meter dash, and now it was time for the next 100-meter dash, but there were two more.

With Summer S.T.E.M. Camp on my mind, I knew what it took to create a curriculum with fun lesson plans that the students would love and interact with through team effort due to challenging material! My goal was to see young students on the way to college by 12 and 13. They should get an early start in life and be the innovators they need to be through action learning, financial literacy, and Science, Technology, Engineering, and

Mathematics. Through Daley Smith Inc., our goal is to expose 500,000 students to S.T.E.M. in five years where they will be given the tools to understand the concepts of action learning, innovation and be efficient at mathematics and be able to choose a S.T.E.M. field upon choice, without equivocation or lack of tools and resources. The goal is for all students to believe in their capabilities and truly live out Philippians 4:13. They will be limitless with regards to their abilities and capacities due to their confidence and the resources and tools given them through the DaleySmith S.T.E.M. program. Their confidence and I.Q.'s will continue to soar through the roof.

Upon creating the perfect summer camp experience, there were some logistics required. I needed to find a place to hold my S.T.E.M. Camp. All locations I researched and called were reasonable; however, these locations were on the other side of the George Washington Bridge, a toll I wasn't willing to pay each day for 24 days. "Next!" I said to myself. There were other properties near me; however, what they were asking for in terms of staff I knew was a big ask given the timeframe, but nothing was going to stop me! The camp was scheduled for July 12 – August 20, 2021. There was a condo-style apartment available on the second floor of my home, and I asked the landlord if she would invest in the program by lending me her apartment for six weeks. She said yes! I had reached out to 800 people on my phone via WhatsApp; I posted on Instagram and made calls to about 50 churches. I put in the work. I also priced the program at an affordable price. There was no way folks weren't going to be a part of this great movement. A friend volunteered her daughter to be a part of the program as a counselor, and she was stellar. On her way to law school that summer, a friend also volunteered as a S.T.E.M. staff member for the program. And one person decided to sponsor one student for the camp! We held about three prayer nights with various teams asking for the blessings of God on this program. Man, was it amazing!

On the first day of S.T.E.M. camp, I was hoisting the tent by myself. My intern and her mom walked in to help. We pitched this lovely strong white tent in the backyard. A few hours passed by, and we realized that no one was under the tent. Where were all the students I had worked so hard for? Where was the next generation of engineers, scientists, aerospace leaders, and S.T.E.M. professionals? Immediately, I got on the phone. Another three days passed, and it was time to do some analysis and calls. At this point, I had two sets of parents with children starting the second week of camp. What a relief, I had designed a quality S.T.E.M. program that they wanted to be a part of! We were teaching math and science through roller skating. The students enjoyed learning about physics, friction, momentum, free body diagrams, and how to roller skate. I enjoyed this time together, and so did the students. We went to a S.T.E.M. roller skating day camp in New Jersey, where they learned about the construction of a rink, soundwaves, and how to create a budget for the sound systems used in rinks. They also learned how to play the piano in a short time. We had a graduation, and all the students had Daley Smith S.T.E.M. Camp shirts printed with the corporate logo. But there was one thing, I made a big boo, boo!

Having a big heart leads to growing pains. I went into debt because of my low prices. I priced the camp too low because I was eager to serve. I was now $3,000 in debt from supplies and activities. I had one sponsorship for one student who needed it. I wanted students to learn so much that I hadn't valued my product enough or made enough connections to sponsor this project. What do I do now? out of debt? I had worked so hard to ensure that I wouldn't be in debt like this. God, what is happening? This was your plan. This is your vision. Tell me what I need to learn. Who do I need to know? What questions do I need to ask? Where do I need to be humbled? What value must I add? Who do I need to add to this team with such a trajectory, God?

God has provided in the past.
God lined up another opportunity after I quit my job. I said, "Ok, God, you are taking care of me"? I remembered being in debt from out-of-state college tuition fees, and a $53,000 scholarship was given to me to cover the debt. I remembered God working in my

favor in the past. I recalled being on my way to Brooklyn, and a young man hit my car and ran. I chased him down, and God came through and provided the officer with the sympathy to give me the perpetrator's address to take the case before the judge. I said God moved in the past. I thought about jumping into a six-foot-deep pool as a seven-year-old at Sesame place. I wanted to play with the floaty, but my mom saw that I was missing from her hand and immediately knew where to find me as I jumped up to gasp for air. I said, "God, I saw you in the past." I thought about when I went to the motherland, and my sister was going to Ethiopia the same week, and I accompanied her there. I saw God lead me in the past, like a sponsor to underwrite my Executive Education Yale Negotiation class during the pandemic. I believe you will do it! again

Reaching internally and asking God for the fire to continue to grow and be limitless as he is, is the message that continues to permeate my mind. I met with Dr. Ranelli Williams at the Baltimore Harbor in Maryland in 2013 as she was on her journey pursuing her doctorate. She said, "Joanna, this is a serious seed, and God is going to do some amazing things in this season"! I continued to see Dr. Ranelli blow up on the internet through the gift of finance and business. She has been transforming lives. I reminded myself of what she told me in 2013, to look at the harvest. You are reading an excerpt because of the vision God gave her and because of the vision God has given me. Stay in tune with God for the vision and purpose He has given you. Remember, you can do anything because God has already given you the strength, Philippians 4:13. Also, keep in mind it is always great to do good. You will reap a reward if you faint not.

Joanna Smith

Joanna Smith is the Founder of the EdTech Company, Daley Smith Inc. She is a professional pianist and an expert in teaching students of all ages. She has been playing piano since the age of four and was taught by the late Ms. Nemhard. She is also a civil engineer who enjoys blending music and mathematical concepts. She has played for 4-star General William "Kip" Ward upon meeting him during her internship in Wiesbaden, Germany. She has also played for the welcome party of Robin A. Kemper, President of the American Society of Engineers. She has created the dynamic annual six-week SUMMER STEM Program with her team to expose 500,000 students to fields in coding, electrical, and mechanical engineering through roller skating. Music and Mathematics are universal languages that Joanna teaches and have allowed her to have such a diverse and strong network worldwide.

You can connect with Joanna on YouTube- Joanna Smith, Exploring Life's Options; her website: www.daleysmithinc.com; and email at **Daleysmithinc@gmail.com**

If God Said It Believe It
By Tina M. Wess

Jesus said unto him, "If thou canst believe, all things are possible to him that believeth."
Mark 9:23

I am standing on the promises of God with Jeremiah 29:11, Galatians 1:15-24, and Mark 9:23 because in God's word, "Jesus said to him, "If thou canst believe, all things are possible to him that believeth." I have referenced several scriptures, but the one I am standing on is Mark 9:23, and my interpretation of that scripture is, "God said it, I believe it that settles it. I believe the most important part of what is implied by the saying is that "God said it." And this is the implication because the Bible is the "Word of God." The problem some people find with the Bible is that both the Old and New Testaments contain these laws and regulations that are laid out; however, especially in the Old Testament, some aren't applicable anymore and don't make sense in light of Christ's revelation. Therefore, some find it difficult to say, "God said it," or, "the Bible says it," and "that settles it." Let's explore.

Dear God,

As I sit and pen this letter to you, I am reminded of how David and Paul penned letters to you. I am standing on your promises, and all your promises are yes and amen. As your word states in the King James Version of Mark 9:23, "Jesus said unto him If thou canst believe, all things are possible to him that believeth.'" This verse, along with your other promises, stand out to me.

When I went through my health challenge in 2017, you spoke your word to me like my girlfriend was holding a conversation with me. It was that plain and clear. You will go through some things, but you will not get consumed. I took you at your word and knew that this was only a season of my life that I had to go through.

God, I thank you for never failing me and keeping your promises to me. During the season of my health challenge, you reminded me that I said in 2010 that I wanted to retire from my job when I was 55. In 2017 I would turn 50, so that meant I would be able to take you at your word and retire in five years. I was in a countdown mode and had one and a half years before retirement. Due to the health challenge, it was delayed by half a year but not denied because I was off on disability for six months, and my state time stopped accruing during this time. As promised, I am looking to retire in June 2023.

God, I thank you for being faithful when I was faithless. I thank you, God, that you are not a man, and you shall not lie. If you said it, I believe and stand on your word and wait on the manifestations in my life. God, even when I lost hope, you were my hope for tomorrow and my joy in the time of sorrow. You know my life story and everything that I have endured that would have taken another out. But because I am grounded and rooted in you and stand on your word, you have seen me through and keep on seeing me through.

I believe the word as spoken in Mark 9:23; "If thou canst believe, all things are possible to him that believeth." God, I take you at your word because, in your word, you said that "your word shall not return until you void it **shall** accomplish what you sent it out to do." Father, you tell us to put your word back on you, and when I need you, I put your word back on you because it shall not return until you void. People look at me and think what they want, but I know I am seated and rooted in your word. I try to live my life as your daughter. I shall have what I decree. I believe it belongs to me.

Whatever God has decreed to you, speak it into the atmosphere. Lord, I am speaking over my home, finances, health, kids, and grandchild. You said in your word that there shall be no lack. Father, I just thank you for being a good daddy, looking beyond my faults, and supplying all my needs. You said you have never seen your seed hungry or begging for bread, and thank you, Father, that I have not. You also say in your word that we have not because we ask not. I am asking you to keep the promise of retirement at age 55 and a half and that I will not only continue to survive but thrive. You are rich in houses and land, and so am I as your child.

Thank you, Father, for never leaving me alone when I left you. Thank you, Father, for always keeping your word to me even when I don't always keep my word to you. God, I am glad that you are not a man, and you shall not lie. I take you at your word and live this life so that I can live it again. Please God, help my unbelief. I have seen your glory and firsthand knowledge that you are real. You saved my life when man said I should have died. For that, I am eternally grateful to you and your promises of yes and amen.

In closing, God, I want to thank you for always loving me when I didn't love myself. Thank you for showing me that I am your daughter, and you are my daddy. No matter what the world says, what does your word say about me? In your son, Jesus' name, Amen.

I was on a training and development assignment with the Business Process Innovation Team as an analyst for a one to two-year assignment. I had just gotten the position in December of 2016, before having my health challenge. When I returned; the manager advised me that he would try to get me to stay on to make up for the five months I had missed while I was out on disability. When I returned to work, everyone told me how they couldn't believe what had happened because I didn't look like what I had been through. I said, well, believe it because I did. I went on several interviews in Sacramento, but I did not get hired. God said, "it is not that you are not capable. It is not time."

In 2018 I came to my current office and interviewed for a position and didn't get it. By this time, I had been on several interviews and was getting discouraged. I prayed, and God said, "my promises are yes and amen, and don't ever forget that. When the position is for you, you will be granted the opportunity." I said, "ok, God, I trust you." After all of my interviews, I received feedback from the panel so I would know what areas to improve for the next interview. One of the managers on the panel told me I did an excellent job and that the office would have more openings, and she highly recommended that I apply again.

In 2019 I applied and was granted an interview. In April of 2019, I relocated to Sacramento to enjoy my promotion and the position I have been in for two years as of April 2021. I am growing and learning a lot. My first year of probation felt like a living hell, but I made it and passed my probation with God's grace and guidance. If you know anything about the public sector, once you have passed probation, it almost takes an act of Congress to get you removed. This part of the retirement plan was in motion. I was on my countdown to retirement at 55.5. I didn't care what happened. Nothing was going to deter me from my goal of retiring at age 55. Even in my current position, I am not settling. Being in Sacramento is a bonus because this is the home of all State jobs.

During my first year of probation, I was focused on passing because I did not have the nicest manager in the world. I was not applying for jobs, but after I passed probation, I started looking for other opportunities because I am standing on God's promise of retiring at age 55.5. If He said it, then I believe it. I have been to some interviews this year but to no avail. The position has not been granted to me, but that will not stop me because I stand on the word of God, no matter what. **If God Said It, Then I Believe It.** The only thing I know how to do is take Him at His word and believe it. God has blessed me in ways I can't explain.

Since the pandemic hit in 2020, I have been able to work an unlimited amount of overtime. This has afforded me opportunities to better myself. This is the second book that I am a co-author in, and I get to add author to my list of accomplishments. I am grateful that God saw little ole me and saw something bigger and better in me than I could or would have ever seen in myself. Sometimes I sit and cry when I listen to the song that says, "He saw the best in me when everyone else could only see the worst in me." Another song that comes to mind is the one that says, "God made me who I am." I tell people, "When you get mad, don't get mad at me but get mad at God because he made me who I am."

In conclusion, If God Said I Believe It. After the Spirit whispered to me that I would be just fine, I walked in that promise. 2021 marks four years since the health challenge. God made me a promise, and I didn't think or feel anything less. If you saw me and didn't know what I had been through, you wouldn't know by looking at me. I do not look like what I have been through because there is no residue. I stand on God's promises daily.

During this time, God also reminded me that in 2010 when my daughter graduated from high school, I told my kids I would retire at 55, and they needed to be solid in their education and careers. In September 2017, I went to a retirement meeting and prayed to God to remind Him of His word to me. He said in His word that His word will not return to Him void, that it will accomplish what He sent it out to do, and that He would never leave or forsake me. I am one and a half years away from retirement at age 55.5 due to being out on disability. If God Said It, Then Believe It. Though it may tarry, it will surely come. Take God at His word and when you begin to feel it is not coming to pass, sit, talk with Him, and think to yourself are you doing what it takes to get that promise.

God makes us promises not for Him to be a magician, and poof they come to pass, but God wants us to work while we wait. Are you preparing yourself for your promise from God when it is granted? Are you prepared for what you prayed for? You are waiting on God, but God is waiting on you. You have asked Him to guide your footsteps but are you moving your feet? Work while it is day because when it is night, no man can see and will be able to work. Get it while the getting is good. God can and will, but what are you doing to assist in the manifestation of your dream

(God's promise)? He told us He will give us the desires of our hearts. How bad do you want them? That is up to you to decide.

Tina M. Wess

Tina M. Wess is a motivational speaker and entrepreneur. She is a single mother of three kids, a daughter and twin boys and has one grandchild. Her life as a single mother is her fuel to speak to women who feel their lives cannot be lived as planned, because now they are alone and have dual roles in their household.

She believes she was born with everything needed to live out her purpose. What she has been given is not just for her, so she has to share and touch the lives of others with her God-given skills by sharing her experiences.

Conclusion
By Dr. Ranelli A. Williams, CPA

No More Unclaimed Promises, like many of my other books, were birthed from a personal need as well as a need I saw in the marketplace. When I found myself allowing fear to take control of my life, I was called to write Releasing the Fear & Walking in Faith. When I neglected to walk boldly in my calling and I saw many others falling for that trap, I collaborated with others to write Belief, Boldness, BIG Blessings. When I realized that God's people, including myself, were forgetting what it is to be a good steward, I pulled together The Perfect 7 project, enlightening our reading audience of the seven areas of stewardship they should focus on. Likewise, when I saw in the marketplace that women felt they had to choose between God, family, and business, I decided to create the book Poised & Promises.

What gap do you see needs to be filled that you are sitting back and waiting for someone else to fix? My sister, the call is yours. If you see it, fix it. God promises to guide you through the process. In Isaiah 30:21 (ESV), He says "And your ears shall hear a word behind you, saying, "This is the way, walk in it," when you turn to the right or when you turn to the left. He will show you the way."

I pulled this compilation together because I want you to be clear that you can stand on the promises and see them fulfilled in your life. In John 10:10 (KJV), Jesus declares "The thief cometh not, but for to steal, and to kill, and to destroy; I am come that they might have life, and that they might have it more abundantly." That "they" refers to you and to me. There is an enemy who is all about taking away what God desires for His children but there is

151

also a redeemer who wants us to reap the harvest He promised us and recover all that was stolen from us.

Let me share one more story with you. Several years ago, when the company I worked for was going through a restructure in preparation for acquisition by another company, I faced losing my job. As the sole income source for my family, outside of our very new business venture that my husband was running, I panicked at first but then quickly turned to the scripture for comfort and guidance. One of my managers at the time shared another role that was available in the company and directed me to apply for it. At the same time, another job opening was brought to my attention, and I applied for that as well. One day, as I sat at home waiting on the feedback from the interviews, and after my daily devotion with God, I began searching the internet. I was led to a post which said, "you can have it all." I immediately knew that God was sending me that message and began to rejoice. I did not know what 'all' meant but I knew in my spirit that God was speaking to me. Within minutes, I received a call from HR stating that they had great news, I was being offered both jobs, so it was up to me to choose the one I wanted. Can you just stop right now and praise God for how He shows up in our lives?

Ladies, when God says it, believe it. He has done it in the past for others and for you and He will do it again. So, when your bank account is dry, believe Him for prosperity. When your body is raking with pain, trust Him for healing. When your marriage is falling apart, call on Him for restoration. When your business is failing, count on Him to turn things around. Find a scripture that supports overcoming whatever challenge you are facing, stand on that promise, and watch God work. Remember "For no matter how many promises God has made, they are "Yes" in Christ. And so, through him the "Amen" is spoken by us to the glory of God (2 Corinthians 1:20, NIV).

Be bold in your stance as you declare "No More Unclaimed Promises."

Dr. Ranelli A. Williams, CPA is passionate about service and helping individuals create breakthrough in their lives and business. She is a Certified Public Accountant, profit strategist, money breakthrough business coach, best-selling author, and award-nominated speaker, empowering service-based entrepreneurs to take control of their money as they work towards building a strong financial legacy.

In addition, Dr. Ranelli is Co-Founder with her husband, Eric Williams of ERJ Services (www.erjservices.com) where in the main arm of the business they help marketing agencies, consultants, and coaches gain clarity and confidence around their business finances, so they are empowered to make strategic decisions for profitability and exponential growth.

Dr. Ranelli also founded R.A.W. Legacy Solutions (www.rawlegacysolutions.com) with the mission of providing mindset and money solutions and support to help Christian female professionals transitioning to full-time entrepreneurship increase cashflow and profits, so they can not only run the cash-rich and profitable businesses they care about, but also build a debt-free legacy and generational wealth.

Made in the USA
Columbia, SC
06 February 2022

55561217R00085